IMMIGRATING TO CANADA

AND FINDING EMPLOYMENT

A 3 IN 1 PUBLICATION

A DO-IT- YOURSELF KIT FOR SKILLED WORKER UNDER LATEST
IMMIGRATION POLICY

A STEP-BY-STEP SETTLEMENT AND JOB SEARCH GUIDE

by

Tariq Nadeem

Co-editors: Noman Nadeem & M. Akram Ghouri

i

ISBN: 0-9733140-2- 8 (Paperback)
ISBN: 0-9733140-3- 6 (e-book)

This book is printed on acid free paper.

Printed in the United States of America
La Vergne, TN and United Kingdom Milton Keynes by arrangements with Self-help publishers Canada

Portions of this book have been provided courtesy of Citizenship and Immigration Canada. The Government of Canada does not endorse or support any annotations or commentary included in this publication. These are the sole responsibility and choice of the author.

Acknowledgement

Statistics Canada information is used with the permission of Minister of Industry, as Minister responsible for Statistics Canada. Information on the availability of the wide range of data from Statistics Canada can be obtained from Statistics Canada's Regional Offices, its World Wide Web site at http://www.statcan.ca and its toll-free access number 1-800-263-1136

Cultural Shock is adopted from an article on introduction to KSA from an unknown source.

Disclaimer

CONTENTS

x

Foreword

Migrating from one country and culture to another is very big move in anyone's life. This publication is my humble effort to save the newcomer's hard earned money and time. I also wish to give the prospective immigrants around the world necessary information and tools in advance to plan their new life well before arriving in Canada. Further, I am trying my best to well equip them to meet the new challenges in a professional manner with the courage to face the unexpected.

Our honorable Federal Minister of Immigration and Citizenship, Mr. Denis Coderre is well informed about all the complaints filed by prospective and new immigrants, specially about the unscrupulous immigration consultants, Immigration Canada has thousands of complaints about these consultants. I would like to refer to a news article in the daily Toronto Star dated Sept.7,2002. According to the newspaper, Mr. Coderre used a stopover in Hong Kong and cited horror stories of consultants who urge their clients to lie on their applications, or who falsely claim that extortionate fees often in excess of US$ 10,000 – will guarantee a visa.

Further, I must thank to my beautiful wife for her cooperation in taking care of my kids especially my 2 year old daughter who always like to hit the keyboard when I am at work. Thanks to my TV set as well that kept my daughter busy as I completed this book project from the comfort of my home.

I must thank and appreciate the cooperation of Ms. Christine Way and Ms. Nicole Hudon of Crown Copyright and Licensing who have guided me in a professional manner to obtain the copyright clearance.

I would also like to thank Mr. Abdul Khaliq, a CGA who taught me the Canadian way of business and accounting, and whose encouragement helped me a lot to complete this publication.

I hope you would like what you have in your hands. *Thanks for checking it out!*

Why Choose Canada?

Canada has a long tradition of welcoming immigrants. Home to two official languages, English and French, Canada is also a multicultural society, with more than 17% of the population reporting a mother tongue other than English or French. During the 1990s, Canada received between 200,000 and 250,000 immigrants per year. In 2001, Canada actually exceeded its target for the first time in years with 250,346 newcomers being granted permanent resident status. This limit will be increased up to 300,000 per year to offset Canada's aging population to synchronize it to 1% of the total population.

50% of all the newcomers come to Toronto, 15% go to Vancouver and 11% to Montreal. Canada is rich, according to World Wealth Report 2001 by Cap Gemini Ernst & Young, **31% of the world's millionaires live in North America** while 4% in Middle East, 24% in Asia Pacific, 36% in Europe and 1% in Africa. Canadians pay $138 Billion every year through their credit card for their shopping.

UN says Canada is the best country in the world!

The United Nations has rated Canada several times the top country in the world for overall quality of life. Canadians enjoy a comfortable standard of living, good health care, social security, a high level of education, and a relatively safe and clean environment. The *Charter of Rights and Freedoms* entrenched in the Canadian constitution guarantees such fundamental rights as equality, mobility and legal rights, as well as freedom of speech, assembly and association.

A 1997 survey of people in 20 countries found that the majority placed Canada in the top ten list of countries where they would like to live. Most consider Canada a generous, peaceful and compassionate nation, while they see Canadians as honest, friendly and polite.

Few facts about Canada

Canada is a land of great natural beauty, from the rugged shores of Newfoundland to the mild climate and beautiful mountains of the west coast. The largest country in the world, it has six time zones. With its coasts, vast forests, mountain ranges, lakes and expanses of prairies, Canada is rich in natural resources. It contains 38 national parks, more than 1000 provincial parks, and nearly 50 territorial parks.

Based on the 1996 census data:

- about 28% of the population reported origins other than British Isles, French or Canadian

- recent immigrants had higher levels of education than the Canadian-born population

- six out of ten households owned their own home

- university or other post-secondary graduates represented 40% of the population over the age of 15

Canadian Students Performance.

Canadian students among top in world survey. They are ranked fourth over-all in UNICEF report. Results reflect that immigrants do better in Canada then any other developed country offering immigration. According to UNICEF report following are the educational performance ranking in reading, math and science among 24 developed nations. They are the members of organization for economic cooperation.

1. South Korea
2. Japan
3. Finland
4. **Canada**
5. Australia
6. Austria
7. United Kingdom
8. Ireland
9. Sweden
10. Czech Republic
11. New Zealand
12. France
13. Switzerland
14. Belgium
15. Iceland
16. Hungary
17. Norway
18. United States
19. Germany
20. Denmark
21. Spain
22. Italy
23. Greece
24. Portugal

Source: Canadian press

ONTARIO BUDGET 2002-03

REVENUE

The projected revenue is $66,544,000,000.
Here's where each budget dollar come from.

Government of Canada

Canada Health & Social Transfer	10.0 ¢
Other Federal	2.0 ¢

Income from Government Enterprises

Lottery & Gaming Corp.	3.7 ¢
Liquor Control Board of Ontario	1.5 ¢
Ontario Power Generation Inc. & Hydro One	0.8 ¢

Other Revenue

Vehicle/Driver Registration fees	1.0 ¢
Liquor Licence Board of Ontario	1.0 ¢
Other Revenue	7.0 ¢

Taxation Revenue

Other Taxes	4.0 ¢
Gasoline & fuel taxes	4.0 ¢
Employer health tax	6.0 ¢
Corporation tax	9.0 ¢
Retail sales tax	21.0 ¢
Personal Income tax	29.0 ¢

EXPENSES 2002-03

How a budget dollar is spent.

Social services	12.0 ¢
Justice	4.0 ¢
General Government	3.0 ¢
Environment resources & economic dev.	9.0 ¢
Public debt interest	14.0 ¢
Education	19.0 ¢
Health	39.0 ¢

Source: Canadian Press

Population of census metropolitan areas

	1997	1998	1999	2000	2001
	thousands				
Toronto (Ontario)	4,499.0	4,586.7	4,669.3	4,763.2	4,881.4
Montréal (Quebec)	3,408.9	3,423.9	3,447.6	3,474.9	3,511.8
Vancouver (British Columbia)	1,967.6	1,998.4	2,028.4	2,058.7	2,078.8
Ottawa–Hull (Ontario–Quebec)	1,045.5	1,055.6	1,068.6	1,086.1	1,107.0
Calgary (Alberta)	873.2	903.0	926.1	947.3	971.5
Edmonton (Alberta)	897.3	914.3	928.1	941.8	956.8
Québec (Quebec)	685.4	686.6	688.4	690.5	693.1
Winnipeg (Manitoba)	677.8	677.8	679.7	682.1	684.8
Hamilton (Ontario)	650.4	657.8	664.7	672.2	680.6
London (Ontario)	413.1	415.9	418.5	422.1	426.3
Kitchener (Ontario)	402.1	408.5	415.5	423.2	431.7
St. Catharines–Niagara (Ontario)	385.5	387.5	388.8	390.9	393.1
Halifax (Nova Scotia)	345.3	348.9	352.8	355.9	359.2
Victoria (British Columbia)	317.6	316.8	317.0	317.1	318.8
Windsor (Ontario)	291.6	295.9	300.6	306.8	313.8
Oshawa (Ontario)	282.0	287.5	292.4	298.9	305.3
Saskatoon (Saskatchewan)	227.6	229.5	230.7	231.0	230.5
Regina (Saskatchewan)	199.1	199.2	199.8	199.3	198.1
St. John's (Newfoundland and Labrador)	176.5	175.2	175.3	175.8	176.2
Chicoutimi–Jonquière (Quebec)	162.7	162.6	161.9	160.5	158.7
Sudbury (Ontario)	163.9	162.0	159.4	158.1	156.7
Sherbrooke (Quebec)	151.3	152.3	152.6	153.6	154.9
Trois-Rivières (Quebec)	142.2	141.9	141.9	141.6	141.5
Thunder Bay (Ontario)	128.5	127.5	126.9	125.8	124.6
Saint John (New Brunswick)	127.9	127.5	127.6	127.7	128.1
1. On July 1 of each year.					
Source: Statistics Canada, CANSIM II, table 051-0014 and Catalogue no 91-213-XIB					
Last modified: September 19, 2002.					

www.statcan.ca/english/Pgdb/People/Population/demo23a.htm

Recent immigrants by country of last residence

	1996-1997	1997-1998	1998-1999	1999-2000	2000-2001
	number of immigrants				
Total immigrants	224,881	193,452	173,210	205,711	252,088
Africa	14,218	13,443	14,303	16,790	22,750
Asia	148,188	117,089	100,433	126,095	156,550
India	20,736	17,427	15,006	21,203	29,139
Hong Kong	29,436	12,522	2,647	1,115	801
Vietnam	1,902	1,860	1,473	1,560	1,789
Philippines	11,921	9,467	8,048	9,390	13,318
Other Asian countries	84,193	75,813	73,259	92,827	111,503
Australasia[2]	1,319	1,344	831	881	1,107
Europe	37,523	39,853	37,907	39,961	45,627
Great Britain	5,452	4,228	4,145	4,830	5,208
France	2,861	3,248	3,969	4,095	4,580
Germany	2,250	1,998	2,453	2,940	1,902
Netherlands	999	646	768	903	882
Greece	292	267	249	249	371
Italy	555	528	436	449	528
Portugal	708	605	343	384	443
Poland	1,863	1,545	1,324	1,351	1,231
Other European countries	22,543	26,788	24,220	24,760	30,482
United States, West Indies	13,895	12,299	11,271	12,387	14,079
United States	5,467	4,709	5,075	5,747	6,030
West Indies	8,428	7,590	6,196	6,640	8,049
Other North and Central American countries	3,457	3,161	2,628	2,971	3,228
South America	5,567	5,535	5,041	5,958	7,754
Other countries	714	728	796	668	993
1. From July 1 of one year to June 30 of the next year.					
2. Australasia includes Australia, Nauru, New Zealand and Papau New Guinea.					
Source: Statistics Canada, CANSIM II, table 051-0006.					
Last modified: June 19, 2002.					

http://cansima.statcan.ca/cgi-win/CNSMCGI.EXE

Population by mother tongue, 1996 Census

	Canada	Quebec	Ontario	Manitoba	Saskatchewan
	Number				
Total Population	28,528,125	7,045,080	10,642,790	1,100,295	976,615
Single responses[1]	28,125,560	6,944,160	10,470,490	1,081,575	962,815
English	16,890,615	586,435	7,694,635	813,055	816,955
French	6,636,660	5,700,150	479,285	47,665	19,075
Non-official languages	4,598,290	657,580	2,296,570	220,855	126,785
Chinese	715,640	40,520	328,165	9,925	6,525
Italian	484,500	130,070	305,155	5,035	895
German	450,140	18,225	159,430	65,295	36,960
Polish	213,410	18,460	139,635	10,940	3,475
Spanish	212,890	65,810	100,890	4,175	1,675
Portuguese	211,290	32,615	150,630	7,565	365
Punjabi	201,785	6,935	76,075	4,760	500
Ukrainian	162,695	6,335	50,490	30,505	23,355
Arabic	148,555	58,225	69,210	795	585
Dutch	133,805	3,650	71,675	4,285	2,250
Tagalog (Pilipino)	133,215	7,800	67,920	15,230	1,580
Greek	121,180	43,035	64,945	1,220	1,235
Vietnamese	106,515	21,620	48,815	2,160	1,625
Cree	76,840	10,730	5,465	23,620	21,090
Inuktitut (Eskimo)	26,960	7,685	165	40	10
Other non-official languages	1,198,870	185,865	657,905	35,305	24,660
Multiple responses[2]	402,560	100,920	172,300	18,720	13,800
English and French	107,945	50,585	33,935	2,540	1,405
English and non-official language	249,545	16,430	130,730	15,820	12,130
French and non-official language	35,845	28,140	5,335	295	190
English, French and non-official language	9,225	5,760	2,300	75	70
– nil or zero					
Source: Statistics Canada, 1996 Census *Nation* tables					

www.statcan.ca/english/Pgdb/People/Population/demo18b.htm

Population by religion, 1981 and 1991 Censuses, Canada

	1981		1991	
	number	%	number	%
Total population	**24,083,495**	**100.0**	**26,994,045**	**100.0**
Catholic	11,402,605	47.3	12,335,255	45.7
Roman Catholic	11,210,385	46.5	12,203,620	45.2
Ukrainian Catholic	190,585	0.8	128,390	0.5
Other Catholic	1,630	--	3,235	--
Protestant	9,914,575	41.2	9,780,715	36.2
United Church	3,758,015	15.6	3,093,120	11.5
Anglican	2,436,375	10.1	2,188,110	8.1
Presbyterian	812,105	3.4	636,295	2.4
Lutheran	702,900	2.9	636,205	2.4
Baptist	696,845	2.9	663,360	2.5
Pentecostal	338,790	1.4	436,435	1.6
Other Protestant	1,169,545	4.9	2,127,190	7.9
Islam	98,165	0.4	253,260	0.9
Buddhist	51,955	0.2	163,415	0.6
Hindu	69,505	0.3	157,010	0.6
Sikh	67,715	0.3	147,440	0.5
Eastern Orthodox	361,565	1.5	387,395	1.4
Jewish	296,425	1.2	318,065	1.2
Para-religious groups	13,450	0.1	28,155	0.1
No religious affiliation	1,783,530	7.4	3,386,365	12.5
Other religions	24,015	0.1	36,970	0.1
-- amount too small to be expressed				
Source: Statistics Canada, Catalogue no. 93-319-XPB.				

www.statcan.ca/english/Pgdb/People/Population/demo32.htm

Expenditures of Canadians in the top 15 countries visited

	2000		
	Overnight visits		
Country visited	Spending in country	Visits	Nights spent
	C$ millions	thousands	
U.S.A.	8,975	14,648	103,024
United Kingdom	974	803	9,617
Mexico	716	731	7,451
France	561	442	4,455
Italy	332	211	2,578
Germany	234	277	2,332
Cuba	210	273	2,366
Japan	191	124	1,636
Spain	172	132	1,946
Dominican Republic	152	195	1,737
Netherlands	115	154	1,341
Republic of Ireland	115	97	1,025
Switzerland	97	124	916
Austria	65	88	515
Belgium	52	93	549
1. Table based on top 15 countries visited (visits).			
Source: Statistics Canada, Culture, Tourism and the Centre for Education Statistics.			
Last modified: novembre 6, 2001.			

www.statcan.ca/english/Pgdb/Economy/Finance/Finarts37a.htm

Expenditures of visitors to Canada from the top 15 countries of origin

Country of origin	2000 Overnight trips		
	Spending in Canada	Trips	Nights spent
	C$ millions	thousands	
United States	7,448	15,225	58,649
United Kingdom	1,004	866	9,324
Japan	573	500	3,299
France	425	404	5,198
Germany	413	385	4,732
Taiwan	246	173	2,275
Australia	224	160	2,055
Mexico	180	143	1,372
South Korea	175	134	1,104
Netherlands	146	128	1,658
Switzerland	146	104	1,266
Hong Kong	135	137	1,327
China	110	74	978
Italy	105	108	1,048
Israel	73	75	707
1. Table based on top 15 countries of origin (trips).			
Source: Statistics Canada, Culture, Tourism and the Centre for Education Statistics.			
Last modified: novembre 6, 2001.			

www.statcan.ca/english/Pgdb/Economy/Finance/Finarts37b.htm

Infant mortality rates

	1993	1994	1995	1996	1997
			infant mortality rate		
Canada	6.3	6.3	6.1	5.6	5.5
Newfoundland and Labrador	7.8	8.2	7.9	6.6	5.2
Prince Edward Island	9.1	6.4	4.6	4.7	4.4
Nova Scotia	7.1	6.0	4.9	5.6	4.4
New Brunswick	7.2	5.4	4.8	4.9	5.7
Quebec	5.7	5.6	5.5	4.7	5.6
Ontario	6.2	6.0	6.0	5.7	5.5
Manitoba	7.1	7.0	7.6	6.7	7.5
Saskatchewan	8.1	8.9	9.1	8.4	8.9
Alberta	6.7	7.4	7.0	6.2	4.8
British Columbia	5.7	6.3	6.0	5.1	4.7
Yukon	7.9	2.3	12.8	0.0	8.4
Northwest Territories	9.6	14.6	13.0	12.2	10.9

1. The infant mortality rate is calculated as the number of deaths of children less than one year of age per 1,000 live births.

Source: Statistics Canada, Catalogue no. 82F0075XCB

www.statcan.ca/english/Pgdb/People/Health/Health21.htm

Life expectancy at birth

	Both sexes	Males	Females	Difference
	years			
Canada				
1920-22	59	59	61	2
1930-32	61	60	62	2
1940-42	65	63	66	3
1950-52	69	66	71	5
1960-62	71	68	74	6
1970-72	73	69	76	7
1980-82	75	72	79	7
1990-92	78	75	81	6
1990-92				
Newfoundland and Labrador	77	74	80	6
Prince Edward Island	77	73	81	8
Nova Scotia	77	74	80	6
New Brunswick	78	74	81	7
Quebec	77	74	81	7
Ontario	78	75	81	6
Manitoba	78	75	81	6
Saskatchewan	78	75	82	7
Alberta	78	75	81	6
British Columbia	78	75	81	6

Source: Statistics Canada, Catalogue no. 82F0075XCB.

www.statcan.ca/english/Pgdb/People/Health/Health26.htm

Consumer Price Index, cities

All items	1997[2]	1998[2]	1999[2]	2000[2]	2001[2]
			1992 = 100		
St. John's (Nfld.Lab.)	108.1	108.5	110.2	113.2	114.5
Charlottetown (P.E.I.)	106.4	106.2	107.4	111.4	114.2
Halifax (N.S.)	107.1	107.9	109.8	113.2	115.5
Saint John (N.B.)	106.7	107.2	109.0	112.5	114.5
Québec (Que.)	105.7	107.3	108.9	111.3	113.8
Montréal (Que.)	104.8	106.5	108.2	110.7	113.4
Ottawa (Ont.)	109.2	110.1	112.2	115.6	119.3
Toronto (Ont.)	107.9	109.0	111.2	114.5	118.1
Thunder Bay (Ont.)	108.7	109.4	111.3	114.3	117.5
Winnipeg (Man.)	111.5	113.0	115.3	118.1	121.5
Regina (Sask.)	110.8	112.7	114.7	117.7	121.3
Saskatoon (Sask.)	109.7	111.3	113.4	116.3	119.7
Edmonton (Alta.)	108.7	109.7	112.2	115.9	118.4
Calgary (Alta.)	109.7	111.3	114.2	118.4	121.3
Vancouver (B.C.)	109.8	110.4	111.4	113.9	116.0
Victoria (B.C.)	109.7	110.0	111.1	113.0	114.3
Whitehorse (Y.T.)	109.9	111.0	112.1	114.6	116.9
Yellowknife (N.W.T.)	108.3	108.2	109.3	111.2	113.0
1. 1996 classification.					
2. Annual average indexes are obtained by averaging the indexes for the 12 months of the calendar year.					
Source: Statistics Canada, CANSIM II, tables 326-0001 and 326-0002					

www.statcan.ca/english/Pgdb/Economy/Economic/econ45a.htm

13

Exchange rates, interest rates, money supply and stock prices

	1997	1998	1999	2000	2001
	US$ per $ Canadian				
Exchange rate	0.7222	0.6741	0.6731	0.6732	0.6456
	%				
Selected interest rates					
Bank rate (last Wednesday of the month)	3.52	5.10	4.92	5.77	4.31
Prime business loan rate	4.96	6.60	6.44	7.27	5.81
Chartered bank typical mortgage rate					
1 year	5.54	6.50	6.80	7.85	6.14
3 years	6.56	6.77	7.37	8.17	6.88
5 years	7.07	6.93	7.56	8.35	7.40
Consumer loan rate	8.75	9.27	10.25	11.71	10.06
90 day prime corporate paper rate	3.61	5.05	4.94	5.71	3.87
	$ millions				
Money supply					
Gross M1	77,981	86,009	92,555	106,151	118,990
M2	449,161	445,967	458,134	489,505	515,087
M3	576,434	598,291	617,260	666,321	701,776
	1975 = 1000				
Toronto Stock Exchange 300 index	6,458.20	6,757.27	7,059.11	9,607.74	7,731.72

Source: Statistics Canada, CANSIM II, tables 176-0036, 176-0043, 176-0047 and 176-0064; Bank of Canada, *Bank of Canada Review*, Ottawa.

Last modified: June 18, 2002.

www.statcan.ca/english/Pgdb/Economy/Economics/econ13a.htm and
www.statcan.ca/english/Pgdb/Economy/Census/econ100a.htm

Employment in the trade, transportation, storage, communications and other utilities industries.

	1998	1999	2000
	Employees[1] (thousands)		
All industries[2]	11,619.6	11,823.2	12,199.6
Transportation, communication and other utilities	872.8	885.8	908.9
Transportation and storage	488.4	501.4	518.0
Transportation	462.2	475.4	491.4
Air transport	69.5	74.0	75.8
Services incidental to air transport	8.7	10.1	14.3
Railway transport and related services	48.4	50.1	51.9
Water transport	15.5	16.5	18.3
Services incidental to water transport	10.6	11.4	12.0
Truck transport	153.1	152.9	154.3
Public passenger transit systems	80.4	83.2	85.4
Other transportation	76.0	77.2	79.5
Pipeline transport	6.6	6.4	6.7
Storage and warehousing	19.5	19.6	19.8
Communication and other utilities	384.4	384.4	390.9
Communication	261.1	259.3	261.8
Telecommunication broadcasting	41.2	41.3	41.5
Telecommunication carriers	103.0	102.4	104.8
Other telecommunication	2.1	2.2	2.4
Postal and courier service	114.9	113.4	113.0
Utilities	123.3	125.1	129.1
Electric power systems	79.4	80.2	82.1
Gas distribution systems	16.0	16.1	17.2
Water systems	6.7	7.6	8.0
Other utilities	21.2	21.3	21.9
	1998	1999	2000
	employees[1] (thousands)		
Trade	2,153.6	2,201.3	2,273.8
Wholesale trade	731.0	766.3	810.5
Farm products	12.3	14.4	16.9
Petroleum products	28.1	29.2	31.3
Food, beverage, drug and tobacco	114.4	116.9	125.6
Apparel and dry goods	19.2	19.4	20.3
Household goods	20.7	20.8	21.7
Motor vehicles, parts and accessories	68.4	69.6	71.2
Metals, hardware, plumbing, heating and building materials	117.7	123.8	133.5
Machinery, equipment and supplies	233.9	246.0	258.1
Other wholesale products	116.3	126.4	131.9
Retail trade	1,422.6	1,435.1	1,463.3
Food, beverage and drug	481.7	488.5	496.7

Shoes, apparel, fabric and yarn	137.6	135.2	144.6
Household furniture, appliances and furnishing	80.0	82.9	87.0
Automotive vehicles, parts and accessories, sales and service	320.2	322.4	326.4
General retail merchandising	182.9	179.2	173.2
Other retail stores	220.2	226.9	235.3

1. Excludes owners or partners of unincorporated business and professional practices, the self-employed, unpaid family workers, persons working outside Canada, military personnel and casual workers for whom a T4 is not required.

2. Excludes agriculture, fishing and trapping, private household services, religious organizations and the

Source: Statistics Canada, CANSIM II, tables 281-0001 and 281-0005 and Catalogue no 72-002-XPB.

Last modified: June 18, 2002.

www.statcan.ca/english/Pgdb/Economy/Communications/trade03.htm

Average weekly earnings (including overtime) in the trade, transportation, storage, communications and other utilities industries.

	1996	1997	1998	1999	2000
			$		
All industries[2]	586.06	598.26	606.32	610.40	626.45
munication and other utilities	735.32	754.55	766.68	772.49	779.32
Transportation and storage	701.22	723.06	735.04	740.28	748.93
- Transportation	695.00	716.30	729.26	734.02	743.06
Air transport	802.87	815.09	811.69	825.23	833.93
Services incidental to air transport	595.80	543.82	546.12	512.19	499.10
Railway transport and related services	976.73	999.29	992.39	1,004.60	1,012.56
Water transport	813.99	829.83	827.42	836.54	849.04
Services incidental to water transport	833.76	772.60	781.83	752.11	754.77
Truck transport	613.46	637.75	674.63	669.37	683.32
Public passenger transit systems	574.70	625.12	631.14	644.07	658.64
Other transportation	658.79	689.80	693.76	700.36	704.67
Pipeline transport	1,157.94	1,187.97	1,221.89	1,352.79	1,368.05
Storage and warehousing	672.80	710.86	707.64	691.66	683.89
Communication and other utilities	776.52	794.50	806.87	814.50	819.59
- Communication	696.05	708.80	704.25	710.87	711.57
Telecommunication broadcasting	835.32	839.06	829.18	833.56	829.41
Telecommunication carriers	843.44	862.83	858.16	840.87	831.33
Other telecommunication	621.17	574.58	634.66	639.91	638.36
Postal and courier service	511.64	518.80	522.67	550.10	558.77
Utilities	941.87	970.39	1,024.23	1,029.23	1,038.53
Electric power systems	1,024.06	1,052.76	1,141.68	1,143.55	1,152.29
Gas distribution systems	885.92	936.34	940.98	967.77	967.36
Water systems	781.10	786.66	797.43	789.90	813.52

	1996	1997	1998	1999	2000
Other utilities	662.36	707.56	719.01	730.90	749.86
Trade	439.72	451.89	467.77	472.56	476.48
Wholesale trade	628.45	643.96	664.37	661.82	663.52
Farm products	518.74	527.87	560.53	591.86	616.33
Petroleum products	626.05	683.30	724.16	708.57	700.72
Food, beverage, drug and tobacco	581.75	587.90	606.18	599.80	576.11
Apparel and dry goods	499.60	544.45	570.24	531.24	535.17
Household goods	658.40	634.91	627.55	601.18	621.11
Motor vehicles, parts and accessories	625.13	650.61	670.79	697.12	709.00
Metals, hardware, plumbing, heating and building materials	585.87	592.97	605.15	608.36	611.83
- Machinery, equipment and supplies	710.87	728.79	745.53	737.94	734.42
Other wholesale products	582.19	599.72	633.22	631.13	659.83
Retail trade	348.06	355.22	366.75	371.50	372.87
Food, beverage and drug	313.23	317.95	324.62	323.51	314.09
Shoes, apparel, fabric and yarn	263.90	267.26	280.82	292.98	296.07
Household furniture, appliances and furnishing	391.54	416.15	435.03	443.00	444.50
- Automotive vehicles, parts and accessories, sales and service	482.76	500.53	520.35	522.31	535.22
General retail merchandising	283.80	294.38	297.52	306.41	304.45
Other retail stores	324.86	315.61	321.96	332.65	342.86

1. Excludes owners or partners of unincorporated business and professional practices, the self-employed, unpaid family workers, persons working outside Canada, military personnel and casual workers for whom a T4 is not required.

2. Excludes agriculture, fishing and trapping, private household services, religious organizations and the military.

Source: Statistics Canada, CANSIM II, tables 281-0002 and 281-0006 and Catalogue no 72-002-XPB.

Last modified: June 18, 2002.

www.statcan.ca/english/Pgdb/Economy/Communications/trade04.htm

17

Imports and exports of goods on a balance-of-payments basis.

	1996	1997	1998	1999	2000	2001
	\$ millions					
Exports	**280,079.3**	**303,378.2**	**326,180.7**	**365,233.2**	**422,558.7**	**413,109.8**
United States[1]	222,461.3	242,542.3	269,335.8	309,193.7	359,551.2	351,085.0
Japan	12,423.4	11,925.5	9,639.9	9,552.0	10,312.3	9,362.8
United Kingdom	4,608.5	4,689.5	5,235.0	5,672.2	6,700.4	6,454.0
Other European Economic Community countries	12,796.3	13,260.4	13,758.4	13,653.5	15,408.6	15,453.2
Other OECD[2]	5,087.8	8,849.0	8,889.9	8,986.5	10,171.1	10,296.3
Other countries[3]	22,702.0	22,111.6	19,321.6	18,175.4	20,415.2	20,458.4
Imports	**2**	**2**	**3**	**326,843.7**	**363,281.3**	**350,502.8**
United States[1]	180,010.1	211,450.8	233,759.1	249,331.2	267,674.5	255,086.9
Japan	7,227.4	8,711.0	9,663.3	10,588.8	11,713.9	10,585.0
United Kingdom	5,581.1	6,126.5	6,083.1	7,689.3	12,256.7	11,830.2
Other European Economic Community countries	14,994.7	18,112.9	19,149.0	0,739.4	21,171.2	23,212.2
Other OECD[2]	9,040.6	11,376.7	11,392.4	13,253.0	18,946.7	18,609.8
Other countries[3]	20,834.6	21,948.7	23,331.2	25,242.0	31,518.3	31,178.8
Balance	**42,390.7**	**25,651.7**	**22,802.7**	**38,389.5**	**59,277.4**	**62,607.0**
United States[1]	42,451.2	31,091.5	35,576.7	59,862.5	91,876.7	95,998.1
Japan	5,196.0	3,214.5	-23.4	-1,036.8	-1,401.6	-1,222.2
United Kingdom	-972.6	-1,437.0	-848.1	-2,017.1	-5,556.3	-5,376.2
Other European Economic Community countries	-2,198.4	-4,852.5	-5,390.6	-7,085.9	-5,762.6	-7,759.0
Other OECD[2]	-3,952.8	-2,527.7	-2,502.5	-4,266.5	-8,775.6	-8,313.5
Other countries[3]	1,867.4	162.9	-4,009.6	-7,066.6	-11,103.1	-10,720.4

1. Includes also Puerto Rico and Virgin Islands.

2. Organisation for Economic Co-operation and Development excluding the United States, Japan, United Kingdom and the other European Economic Community.

3. Countries not included in the European Economic Community or the OECD.

Source: Statistics Canada, CANSIM II, tables 228-0001, 228-0002 and 228-0003.

Last modified: June 18, 2002.

www.statcan.ca/english/Pgdb/Economy/International/Gblec02a.htm

18

Average weekly earnings[1] (including overtime), finance and other service industries

	1996	1997	1	1	2
			$		
	586.06	598.26	606.32	610.40	626.45
Finance, insurance and real estate	704.59	742.17	754.62	760.72	777.52
Finance and insurance	749.68	784.89	801.84	804.57	824.63
Deposit accepting intermediaries	632.38	659.69	686.83	704.02	732.01
Banks	656.87	667.45	684.92	705.90	729.90
Trust companies	624.82	662.04	692.85	704.40	722.19
Deposit accepting mortgage companies	739.78	x	x	x	x
Credit unions	553.14	628.22	684.80	691.74	733.40
Consumer and business financing intermediaries	777.69	810.14	811.37	786.71	764.20
Investment intermediaries	798.83	786.36	741.46	715.64	676.07
Insurance (excluding agencies)	787.64	827.68	889.69	910.79	902.73
Other financial intermediaries	1,468.56	1,604.65	1,485.73	1,296.21	1,348.26
Real estate operator and insurance agencies	587.18	631.67	632.67	643.28	648.95
Business services	651.93	680.50	687.45	698.76	731.37
Employment agencies and personnel suppliers	429.99	473.65	485.34	486.54	498.30
Computer and related services	829.90	888.17	900.77	938.05	977.19
Accounting and bookkeeping services	609.77	631.81	650.95	676.23	698.76
Advertising services	649.21	631.37	605.21	616.89	663.21
Architectural, engineering and other scientific and technical services	847.40	867.12	854.59	854.11	881.53
Offices of lawyers and notaries	657.58	675.19	698.21	699.35	725.34
Management consulting services	691.92	705.97	716.56	728.48	793.64
Other business services	507.55	533.25	533.79	538.31	549.46

	1	1997	1	1	2
			$		
al and related services	671.64	668.38	662.25	658.99	672.88
	509.81	517.52	519.42	525.29	542.25
Accomodation, food and beverage services	236.83	235.36	231.49	235.10	244.44
Accomodation services	307.64	308.78	297.17	302.98	311.74
Food and beverage services	217.28	215.80	213.93	216.96	225.73
Miscellaneous services	405.17	407.35	405.59	410.77	423.68
Amusement and recreational services	389.61	393.30	386.34	397.38	409.84
Personal services (excluding households services)	334.29	336.37	334.02	340.40	350.01
Barber and beauty shops	297.52	294.90	284.74	291.40	305.05

Laundries and cleaners	364.23	367.10	375.65	384.75	382.2(
Funeral services	502.88	515.13	513.09	523.99	556.1ˑ
Other personal and household services	263.50	282.96	289.31	282.99	292.4ˑ
Membership organizations	491.49	486.70	482.04	498.04	514.8
Other services	413.07	413.45	418.26	413.10	428.5ˑ
Auto and trucking rental and leasing services	534.16	525.14	500.09	505.08	523.8ˑ
Photographers	378.28	392.75	412.86	398.15	422.8ˑ
Services to buildings and dwellings	315.51	323.32	321.98	308.39	322.7(
Travel services	513.19	498.56	516.92	494.93	510.8ˑ
Other services	442.96	443.01	453.78	459.03	473.8
Public administration	740.05	739.57	737.53	741.07	760.1ˑ

1. Excludes owners or partners of unincorporated business and professional practices, the self-employed, unpaid family workers, persons working outside Canada, military personnel and casual workers for whom a T4 is not required.

2. Excludes agriculture, fishing and trapping, private household services, religious organizations and the military.

Source: Statistics Canada, CANSIM II, tables 281-0002 and 281-0006 and Catalogue no 72-002-XIB.

st modified: 2002-12-20.

www.statcan.ca/english/Pgdb/Economy/Finance/fin12.htm

Mineral reserves

	1994	19	19	19	1
Crude petroleum (million cubic metres)[1]	1,259.0	1,383.0	1,372.0	1,387.0	1,448.0
Natural gas (billion cubic metres)[1]	2,232.2	1,897.8	1,929.0	1,841.0	1,809.0
Crude bitumen (million cubic metres)[1]	158.8	169.6	197.5	211.1	229.8
Coal (megatonnes)[1]	8,623.0	8,623.0	8,623.0	8,623.0	8,623.0
Copper (thousand tonnes)[2]	9,533.0	9,250.0	9,667.0	9,032.0	8,402.0
Nickel (thousand tonnes)[2]	5,334.0	5,832.0	5,632.0	5,122.0	5,683.0
Lead (thousand tonnes)[2]	3,861.0	3,660.0	3,450.0	2,344.0	1,845.0
Zinc (thousand tonnes)[2]	14,514.0	14,712.0	13,660.0	10,588.0	10,159.0
Molybdenum (thousand tonnes)[2]	148.0	129.0	144.0	149.0	121.0
Silver (tonnes)[2]	19,146.0	19,073.0	18,911.0	16,697.0	15,738.0
Gold (tonnes)[2]	1,513.0	1,540.0	1,510.0	1,724.0	1,415.0
Uranium (thousand tonnes)[3]	397.0	381.0	369.0	331.0	312.0

1. Proved reserves recoverable with present technology and prices

2. Proven and probable reserves

3. Reserves recoverable from mineable ore

Sources: Statistics Canada, catalogue no. 26-201,26-206 and 26-213; Canadian Petroleum Association Statistical Yearbook; Alberta Energy Conservation Board; Natural Resources Canada, Canadian Minerals Yearbook

www.statcan.ca/english/Pgdb/Land/Geography/physo09.htm

Population projections for 2001, 2006.

	2001			2006		
	Both sexes	Male	Female	Both sexes	Male	Female
	thousands			thousands		
All ages[2]	31,002.2	15,348.8	15,653.4	32,228.6	15,947.4	16,281.2
0–4	1,715.9	880.5	835.4	1,640.2	841.4	798.8
5–9	2,026.6	1,038.2	988.4	1,790.4	918.4	872.0
10–14	2,076.6	1,065.5	1,011.0	2,096.4	1,075.8	1,020.6
15–19	2,081.0	1,069.7	1,011.2	2,155.3	1,107.5	1,047.9
20–24	2,097.0	1,070.5	1,026.5	2,167.6	1,105.9	1,061.7
25–29	2,100.3	1,064.1	1,036.2	2,194.1	1,113.3	1,080.8
30–34	2,252.5	1,138.4	1,114.1	2,201.6	1,115.0	1,086.6
35–39	2,641.7	1,332.6	1,309.1	2,326.8	1,172.8	1,154.0
40–44	2,659.1	1,331.6	1,327.6	2,675.7	1,346.9	1,328.9
45–49	2,384.9	1,189.6	1,195.3	2,663.7	1,334.1	1,329.6
50–54	2,114.7	1,053.3	1,061.3	2,362.9	1,175.0	1,187.9
55–59	1,625.9	804.2	821.7	2,073.7	1,024.9	1,048.8
60–64	1,291.1	631.3	659.7	1,578.1	771.6	806.5
65–69	1,137.8	547.6	590.2	1,222.4	586.9	635.5
70–74	1,012.0	464.4	547.6	1,030.5	481.1	549.4
75–79	815.2	339.3	475.9	858.7	374.8	483.9
80–84	525.7	196.7	329.0	627.5	239.6	387.9
85–89	295.2	94.6	200.6	351.3	113.5	237.7
90 and over	149.2	36.3	112.7	211.8	48.9	162.9

1. Figures represent the medium-growth projection and are based on 2000 population estimates.
2. Due to rounding, the totals may not always add up to the sum of the figures.
Source: Statistics Canada, CANSIM, Matrix 6900.

www.statcan.ca/english/Pgdb/People/Population/demo23a.htm

Health care beds, all institutions, by type of care.

	1996-1997			
	Total	Short-term care	Rehabilitation	Extended care[2]
	Number of approved beds[3]			
Canada	352,334	112,872	2,573	46,422
Newfoundland and Labrador	6,996	2,326	–	2,160
Prince Edward Island	2,507	515	–	777
Nova Scotia	12,547	3,350	–	200
New Brunswick	12,830	3,794	20	2,706
Quebec[4]	68,972	32,094	1,373	1,055
Ontario	128,249	32,492	482	19,962
Manitoba	18,146	4,786	–	8,225
Saskatchewan	18,411	6,293	–	4,605
Alberta	38,180	11,048	274	636

British Columbia	44,571	15,776	424	6,046
Yukon	282	110	–	50
Northwest Territories	643	288	–	–

– nil or zero

1. Beds are beds approved by the provincial authorities for facilities with four or more beds in operation at the end of the reporting year.

2. Treatment of patients with long-term illness or with a low potential for recovery and who require regular medical assessment and continuing nursing care.

3. All beds in a facility are counted in the category of the principal type of care of the facility (e.g., all beds of a general hospital with a long-term care unit are counted as short-term care beds).

4. Quebec residential care facilities are not classified by type of care.

Source: Statistics Canada and Canadian Institute for Health Information.

www.statcan.ca/english/Pgdb/People/Health/health32a.htm

Average weekly earnings, health care and social assistance, provinces and territories.

	1997	1998	1999	2000	2001
	$[1]				
Canada	**545.48**	**543.36**	**544.68**	**562.25**	**581.29**
Newfoundland and Labrador	510.29	517.01	572.79	617.40	630.23
Prince Edward Island	504.37	528.40	521.90	542.49	569.18
Nova Scotia	490.01	531.88	508.16	525.72	555.00
New Brunswick	500.25	499.32	499.90	516.99	536.38
Quebec	572.33	545.50	529.55	543.53	562.77
Ontario	556.01	558.75	568.12	585.69	601.94
Manitoba	468.09	478.92	443.22	450.06	469.32
Saskatchewan	469.36	482.62	494.48	506.36	527.61
Alberta	521.70	527.05	543.64	565.06	590.89
British Columbia	556.22	562.87	574.97	595.07	612.51
Yukon	689.04	691.74	639.43	665.81	624.99
Northwest Territories including Nunavut	718.39	738.84	732.72	766.01	827.49

1. Unadjusted for seasonal variation.

Source: Statistics Canada, CANSIM II, table 281-0027 and Catalogue no. 82-221-XIE.

Last modified: January 23, 2002.

www.statcan.ca/english/Pgdb/People/Health/health23.htm

Expenditures on education, by education level.

	1995-1996			
	Canada	Quebec	Ontario	Manitoba
	$ millions			
Education expenditures[1]	58,943.71	14,429.12	22,210.40	2,250.09
Level				
Elementary and secondary	36,424.71	8,147.61	14,964.17	1,551.68
Community college	4,531.82	1,916.03	1,309.46	66.43
University	11,801.98	3,220.86	4,094.97	459.65
Vocational training	6,185.20	1,144.62	1,841.80	172.33
Direct source of funds				
Federal government[2]	6,754.13	1,383.04	1,791.24	378.43
Provincial governments	32,170.93	10,617.98	9,424.71	1,059.48
Municipal governments[3]	12,779.83	765.81	8,197.02	529.69
Fees and other sources	7,238.81	1,662.29	2,797.44	282.48

1. Includes operating, capital, student aid and all departmental expenditures.

2. In addition to the direct funding reported here, the federal government also provides indirect support in respect of postsecondary education to provinces and territories under the Federal-Provincial Fiscal Arrangements and Federal Post-secondary Education and Health Contributions Act, 1977 and under the Official Languages in Education Program.

3. Includes local school taxation.

Source: Statistics Canada, CANSIM, Cross-classified tables 00590203, 00590204, 00590206, 00590305, 00590306

www.statcan.ca/english/Pgdb/People/education/educ14b.htm

Average weekly earnings (including overtime), educational and related services.

	1997	1998	1999	2000
	$			
All industries[2]	598.26	606.32	610.40	626.45
Educational and related services	668.38	662.25	658.99	672.88
Educational services	679.68	672.60	669.55	684.31
Elementary and secondary education	709.18	702.63	696.26	710.14
Postsecondary non-university education	625.26	613.88	631.73	655.05
University education	619.26	612.52	606.99	620.68
Libraries, museums and other educational services	435.84	445.61	446.88	458.45
Library services	412.78	429.57	433.42	436.77
Museums and archives	511.23	524.47	512.59	521.57
Other educational services	408.72	409.20	417.45	434.89

1. Excludes owners or partners of unincorporated businesses and professional practices, the self-employed, unpaid family workers, persons working outside Canada, military personnel, and casual workers for whom a T4 is not required.

2. Excludes agriculture, fishing and trapping, private household services, religious organizations, and the military.

Source: Statistics Canada, CANSIM II, tables 281-0002 and 281-0006.

www.statcan.ca/english/Pgdb/People/education/educ05.htm

Average total income by selected family types.

	1995	1996	1997	1998	1999
	\$ constant 1999				
Economic families[2], two people or more	**58,592**	**59,451**	**60,772**	**63,247**	**63,818**
Elderly families[3]	45,519	42,385	42,813	43,139	45,142
Married couples only	41,210	41,234	41,749	41,984	44,425
All other elderly families	56,651	46,788	46,546	47,328	47,882
Non-elderly families[4]	60,996	62,078	63,582	66,429	66,827
Married couples only	59,010	60,974	63,122	65,100	63,190
No earner	25,294	28,977	29,491	28,563	30,217
One earner	46,656	46,031	49,106	52,164	51,622
Two earners	67,202	70,522	71,509	74,147	71,340
Two parent families with children[5]	65,847	66,188	68,255	71,392	72,910
No earner	18,132	19,946	21,365	20,810	20,569
One earner	46,924	50,144	49,459	55,402	54,407
Two earners	68,467	68,332	70,284	72,749	73,984
Three or more earners	83,714	85,504	87,326	87,665	90,868
Married couples with other relatives[6]	80,957	85,028	85,692	88,536	91,332
Lone-parent families[5]	28,350	28,390	28,366	30,574	30,470
Male lone-parent families	38,690	42,864	41,947	45,151	45,829
Female lone-parent families	26,608	25,938	25,886	27,843	27,571
No earner	15,905	15,075	13,935	14,395	14,993
One earner	29,249	29,966	28,915	29,540	28,927
Two or more earners	44,029	41,163	43,028	46,069	42,494
All other non-elderly families	47,617	54,458	53,442	58,113	56,865
Unattached individuals	**25,634**	**25,414**	**25,431**	**26,289**	**27,058**
Elderly male	25,200	26,150	26,503	26,992	26,609
Non-earner	22,488	23,438	23,673	23,446	24,222
Earner	47,486	45,471	42,337	47,935	40,161
Elderly female	19,874	20,990	21,075	20,785	20,772
Non-earner	19,366	20,143	20,194	19,951	19,994
Earner	32,419	38,704	32,450	31,975	31,557
Non-elderly males	29,032	28,837	28,693	30,221	30,890
Non-earner	11,102	10,234	9,943	9,794	9,858
Earner	32,657	32,793	32,530	33,852	34,505
Non-elderly females	24,832	23,457	23,575	24,322	26,008
Non-earner	12,083	9,713	10,615	10,077	9,597
Earner	28,470	27,746	27,476	28,757	30,978

1. Average total income refers to income from all sources including government transfers and before deduction of federal and provincial income taxes. It may also called income before tax (but after transfers).

2. An economic family is a group of individuals sharing a common dwelling unit who are related by blood, marriage (including common-law relationships) or adoption.

3. Head 65 years of age and over.

4. Head less than 65 years of age.

5. With single children less than 18 years of age. Children 18 years of age and over and/or other relatives may also be present.

6. Children less than 18 years of age are not present, but children 18 years of age and over may be present.

Source: Statistics Canada, Catalogue no. 75-202-XIE.

Last modified: October 25, 2001.

www.statcan.ca/english/Pgdb/People/Families/famil05.htm

Average household expenditures, Canada and provinces.

Household characteristics	2000					
	Canada[1]		Quebec		Ontario	
Number of households in sample	14,250		1,828		1,857	
Estimated number of households	11,361,810		2,930,590		4,210,680	
Average household size	2.57		2.40		2.68	
	Average expenditure per household	Household s reporting expenditur es	Average expenditure per household	Household s reporting expenditur es	Average expenditure per household	Households reporting expenditure s
	$	%	$	%	$	%
Total expenditures	55,834	100.0	48,318	100.0	62,738	100.0
Total current consumption	39,385	100.0	33,758	100.0	43,645	100.0
Food	6,217	100.0	6,073	100.0	6,556	100.0
Shelter	10,498	99.7	8,533	99.8	12,224	99.7
Household operation	2,516	100.0	2,034	99.9	2,834	99.9
Household furnishings and equipment	1,557	93.4	1,218	88.3	1,811	95.3
Clothing	2,351	99.1	2,123	98.7	2,675	99.4
Transportation	7,576	98.0	6,164	96.8	8,476	98.6
Health care	1,357	97.1	1,359	96.8	1,194	96.9
Personal care	740	99.3	722	98.8	810	99.5
Recreation	3,165	97.7	2,553	96.4	3,430	98.1
Reading materials and other printed matter	275	86.3	239	79.8	310	87.9
Education	826	42.5	487	40.5	1,031	40.7
Tobacco products and alcoholic beverages	1,218	84.3	1,302	88.6	1,186	82.9
Games of chance (net amount)	261	74.2	285	80.1	263	72.2
Miscellaneous	827	90.4	665	88.8	843	91.4
Personal income taxes	12,012	90.4	11,131	87.2	13,782	93.3
Personal insurance payments and pension contributions	3,135	80.0	2,690	80.6	3,719	79.6
Gifts of money and contributions	1,302	73.4	739	60.6	1,592	78.8

1. The Canada total excludes data for the Yukon, the Northwest Territories and Nunavut.
Source: Statistics Canada, CANSIM II, table 203-0001.
Last modified: December 4, 2001.

www.statcan.ca/english/Pgdb/People/Families/famil16a.htm

Labour force characteristics (population 15 years and older) by Census metropolitan areas.

| Metropolitan area | 2001 | | | | | | |
	Population	Labour force	Employment	Unemployment	Unemployment rate	Participation rate	Employment rate
			Thousands			%	
St. John's	141.9	94.5	85.9	8.6	9.1	66.6	60.5
Halifax	280.4	197.7	183.8	13.9	7.0	70.5	65.5
St. John	100.6	64.2	58.1	6.1	9.5	63.8	57.8
Chicoutimi-Jonquière	132.4	78.9	70.1	8.8	11.2	59.6	52.9
Québec	568.0	367.8	339.0	28.8	7.8	64.8	59.7
Sherbrooke	125.7	80.7	74.4	6.3	7.8	64.2	59.2
Trois-Rivières	116.8	72.5	65.5	7.0	9.7	62.1	56.1
Montréal	2,826.1	1,857.7	1,705.7	152.0	8.2	65.7	60.4
Ottawa-Hull	875.1	615.0	576.1	39.0	6.3	70.3	65.8
Oshawa	236.7	163.4	154.3	9.2	5.6	69.0	65.2
Toronto	3,951.1	2,745.7	2,571.8	173.8	6.3	69.5	65.1
Hamilton	550.7	371.1	348.3	22.8	6.1	67.4	63.2
St. Catharines-Niagara	321.9	202.7	190.0	12.7	6.3	63.0	59.0
Kitchener	342.1	240.5	225.7	14.8	6.2	70.3	66.0
London	341.1	230.7	216.0	14.7	6.4	67.6	63.3
Windsor	249.9	165.7	154.6	11.1	6.7	66.3	61.9
Sudbury	128.9	79.4	72.5	6.9	8.7	61.6	56.2
Thunder Bay	101.8	67.5	62.1	5.4	8.0	66.3	61.0
Winnipeg	536.9	377.6	358.2	19.4	5.1	70.3	66.7
Regina	156.1	111.3	105.2	6.1	5.5	71.3	67.4
Saskatoon	181.6	123.2	115.6	7.6	6.2	67.8	63.7
Calgary	789.4	596.3	569.5	26.8	4.5	75.5	72.1
Edmonton	752.0	531.1	504.8	26.2	4.9	70.6	67.1
Vancouver	1,712.9	1,125.1	1,051.1	74.0	6.6	65.7	61.4
Victoria	258.1	158.5	148.9	9.6	6.1	61.4	57.7

Source: Statistics Canada, CANSIM II, table 282-0053 and Catalogue no 71-001-PIB.
Last modified: June 19, 2002.

www.statcan.ca/english/Pgdb/People/Labour/Labor35.htm

Employment and average weekly earnings public administration and all industries.

	1997	1998	1999	2000	2001
	Employees[2] (thousands)				
All industries[3]	11,643.2	11,903.5	12,074.8	12,482.8	12,781.2
Public administration	707.6	702.3	705.0	713.0	723.1
Federal administration[4]	236.8	234.7	237.9	240.9	247.5
Provincial and territorial administration	202.7	202.1	206.1	208.0	208.4
Local administration	234.8	231.5	226.6	229.9	232.2
	Average weekly earnings[2] ($)				
All industries[3]	623.23	632.16	638.92	653.60	665.12
Public administration	725.14	725.91	736.71	747.55	752.35
Federal administration[4]	801.45	806.36	813.90	827.16	815.88
Provincial and territorial administration	741.41	750.14	758.82	767.44	780.45
Local administration	666.15	657.34	671.37	680.57	692.52

1. Including overtime.

2. Excludes owners or partners of unincorporated business and professional practices, the self-employed, unpaid family workers, persons working outside Canada, military personnel and casual workers for whom a T-4 is not required.

3. Excludes agriculture, fishing and trapping, private household services, religious organizations and the military.

4. Excludes the military.

Source: Statistics Canada, CANSIM II, tables 281-0024 and 281-0027.

Last modified: June 19, 2002.

www.statcan.ca/english/Pgdb/State/Government/govt18.htm

INTERNATIONAL CONTEXTS

The international environment has changed significantly in the wake of the terrorist attacks in the United States. There is a heightened awareness of the sophistication and geographic reach of terrorist activities, and the need to ensure that Canada's immigration and refugee protection programs are not seen as gateways to these activities in North America.

It is difficult to predict how the current campaign against terrorism will affect the global movement of people. Other factors that influence Canada's ability to attract and process immigrants and non-immigrants in an efficient and timely manner include the following:

- a significant increase in immigrant and non-immigrant applicants to Canada, including refugee claimants;

- a shift in source countries;

- the number of people on the move worldwide; and

- international skilled workers.

About 150 million people are on the move at any given time.

Between 1997 and 2000, the number of immigrant applications increased by 46 percent. Currently, 50 percent more applications have been received than are needed to meet program targets. The growth in non-immigrant applications during those years was unprecedented: applications for visitor visas rose by 27 percent; applications for employment authorizations (temporary work permits) rose by 43 percent; and applications for student authorizations (issued for the most part to post-secondary students) rose by 63 percent. Since 1998, there has also been a significant increase in refugee claims made in Canada, from just under 25,500 in 1998 to more than 35,000 in 2000.
Canada draws its immigrant population from a great number of countries, but over time, we have seen significant shifts in primary source countries. In 1990, the top two source countries were Hong Kong and Poland, which together accounted for some 20 percent of the movement in that year. In 2000, China and India were the two primary source countries, making up close to 30 percent of the movement.

Behind the interest in Canada as a migrant destination is the increasing worldwide mobility of people. It has been estimated that about 150 million people are on the move at any given time. Some flee persecution, civil strife, or severe political or economic upheaval; others are forced to leave as a result of natural disasters or environmental degradation; still others move primarily to seek a better way of life for themselves and their families. In short, migration as an aspect of globalization is accelerating. If it wishes to maximize the benefits of this movement, Canada cannot afford to stand still. We must proactively plan for the future.

The key to sustaining a robust immigration program hinges on striking the right balance between maximizing the benefits of immigration, such as economic growth and social development, and sustaining public confidence in the system by ensuring, through effective enforcement, that its generosity is not abused. Canada is not alone in facing increased pressures from irregular migration, including human trafficking and smuggling.

Currently, Canada, the United States, Australia and New Zealand are the only countries that encourage and plan for immigration. However, greater international economic integration and competition, ageing work forces and declining birth rates are leading countries of the European Union and Japan to reconsider their approach to the planned admission of foreign workers. It is anticipated that in the future, Canada will face serious competition in recruiting the highly skilled as most developed countries struggle with skill shortages and the effects of an ageing population.

How are Immigrants Chosen?

Since this book is designed to focus on skilled worker class immigrants who are the major source of immigration to Canada, so we will only touch other classes but master the skilled worker class.

Immigrating to Canada

Every year, Canada welcomes thousands of new residents to Canada. As someone interested in building a home for yourself in Canada, you have a number of options when applying for permanent residence status. Canada also fulfils its international humanitarian commitments by accepting a certain number of refugees each year. Read about these programs and decide which class suits you and your family best.

Skilled Worker Class Immigration

Canada values the skills and experiences that foreign professionals and workers bring with them. Check to see if your skills and experience qualify you to come to Canada as a skilled worker.

Business Class Immigration

Canada has a strong economic culture. If you have experience running or investing in businesses, you may qualify to come to Canada as a business immigrant. You can learn more by visiting this site.
http://www.cic.gc.ca/english/business/index.html

Who is a Business Immigrant?

Business immigrants are people who can invest in, or start businesses in Canada and are expected to support the development of a strong and prosperous Canadian economy. The Business Immigration Program seeks to attract people experienced in business to Canada.

Business immigrants are selected based on their ability to become economically established in Canada.

There are three classes of business immigrants:

1) Investors

The Immigrant Investor Program seeks to attract experienced persons and capital to Canada. Investors must demonstrate business experience, a minimum net worth of CDN $800,000 and make an investment of CDN $400,000.

2) Entrepreneurs

The Entrepreneur Program seeks to attract experienced persons that will own and actively manage businesses in Canada that will contribute to the economy and create jobs. Entrepreneurs must demonstrate business experience, a minimum net worth of CDN $300,000 and are subject to conditions upon arrival in Canada.

3) Self-employed persons

Self-employed persons must have the intention and ability to create their own employment. They are expected to contribute to the cultural, artistic or athletic life of Canada. They may create their own employment by purchasing and managing a farm in Canada.

Canada has Business Immigration Centres (BICs) specially staffed to assess potential business immigrants. You may wish to mail your application directly to a BIC to obtain a more specialized processing of your application. To do so, mail your completed application to one of the centres in Beijing, Berlin, Buffalo, Damascus, Hong Kong, London, Paris, Seoul and Singapore.

The application forms and guide can be downloaded from this site. *http://www.cic.gc.ca/english/applications/business.html*

Family Class Immigration

Family class immigration reunites families in Canadian homes. Learn how to sponsor your family member or come to Canada as a member of the family class from this website. *http://www.cic.gc.ca/english/sponsor/index.html*

International Adoption

Adopting children from abroad can be a long process. This is to protect children's rights. Learn about what you need to do to bring an adoptive child to Canada. You can learn more by visiting this website. *http://www.cic.gc.ca/english/sponsor/adopt-1.html*

Provincial Nomination

Most provinces in Canada have an agreement with the Government of Canada that allows them to play a more direct role in selecting immigrants who wish to settle in that province. If you wish to immigrate to one of Canada's provinces as a Provincial Nominee, you must first apply to the province where you wish to settle. The province will consider your application based on their immigration needs and your genuine intention to settle there.

Before applying to immigrate to Canada, Provincial Nominees must complete the provincial nomination process. Contact the province for more information.

Provincial Nominee Program - Contact Information

If you wish to come to Canada as a Provincial Nominee, you must first apply to the province to be nominated for immigration. Citizenship and Immigration Canada will process your application for permanent residence after the province sends a Certificate of Provincial Nomination to the Visa Office where you will send your forms.

Contact the provinces for more information on their Provincial Nominee Programs.

Alberta

Provincial Nominee Program
Economic Immigration
Alberta Economic Development
4th Floor, Commerce Place
10155-102 Street
Edmonton, Alberta
T5J 4L6

www.alberta-canada.com/pnp

British Columbia

Provincial Nominee Program
Ministry of Community, Aboriginal & Women's Service
P.O. Box 9915 Stn Prov Gov
Victoria, British Columbia
V8W 9V1

www.pnp.mi.gov.bc.ca

Manitoba

Provincial Nominee Program
Immigration Promotion & Recruitment Branch
Labour and Immigration Manitoba
9th Floor, 213 Notre Dame Avenue
Winnipeg, Manitoba
R3B 1N3

http://www.gov.mb.ca/labour/immigrate/english/immigration/1.html

New Brunswick

Provincial Nominee Program
Training and Employment Development
P.O. Box 6000
Fredericton, New Brunswick
E3B 5H1

www.gnb.ca/immigration/english/index.htm

Newfoundland and Labrador

Provincial Nominee Program
Industry, Trade and Technology
Confederation Building
West Block, 4th Floor
P.O. Box 8700
St. John's, Newfoundland
A1B 4J6

www.gov.nf.ca/itrd/prov_nominee.htm

Nova Scotia

Provincial Nominee Program
The Office of Economic Development
World Trade and Convention Centre
1800 Argyle Street
P.O. Box 519
Halifax, Nova Scotia
B3J 2R7

www.gov.ns.ca

Prince Edward Island

Provincial Nominee Program
Immigration and Investment Division
94 Euston Street, 2nd floor
Charlottetown, Prince Edward Island
C1A 7M8

www.gov.pe.ca

Saskatchewan

Provincial Nominee Program
Dept. of Government Relations and Immigration
Immigration Branch
2nd Floor - 1919 Saskatchewan Drive
Regina, Saskatchewan
S4P 3V7

www.immigrationsask.gov.sk.ca

Yukon

Provincial Nominee Program
Business Immigration, Industry Development
Business, Tourism and Culture
P.O. Box 2703
Whitehorse, Yukon
Y1A 2C6

www.btc.gov.yk.ca

Note: After you have been nominated by a province, you have to make a separate application to Citizenship and Immigration Canada (CIC) for permanent residence. A CIC officer will assess your application on Canadian immigration regulations.

Provincial Nominees **are not** assessed on the six selection factors of the Federal Skilled Workers Program.

Quebec-Selected Immigration

Quebec is responsible for selecting immigrants who wish to settle in Quebec. Find out how to apply to be selected to settle in Quebec.

Immigrating to Quebec
as a Skilled Worker

The Quebec government and the Government of Canada have an agreement that allows Quebec to select immigrants who best meet its immigration needs. Under the Canada-Quebec Accord on Immigration Quebec is able to establish its own immigration requirements and select immigrants who will adapt well to living in Quebec.

To come to Canada as a Quebec Skilled Worker, you must first apply to the Quebec government for a *Certificat de selection du Québec*. Visit the Quebec Immigration Web site for more information http://www.immq.gouv.qc.ca/anglais/how_immigrate/workers/index.html

Note: After you have been selected by Quebec, you have to make a separate application to Citizenship and Immigration Canada (CIC) for permanent residence. A CIC officer will assess your application on Canadian immigration regulations.

Quebec Skilled Workers **are not** assessed on the six selection factors of the Federal Skilled Workers Program.

Immigrating to Canada as a Skilled Worker

Since this book is designed to focus on the Federal Skilled Workers Program which is the major source of immigrants to Canada. (for more detailed facts and figures about this program, visit http://www.cic.gc.ca/english/pdf/pub/facts2001.pdf), so we will try to master every aspect under this category to enable potential candidates to not only evaluate their eligibility but to prepare their immigration application in a professional manner by themselves and save thousands of dollars as professional fee that most of the candidates prefer to pay because of lack of confidence and knowledge.

SKILLED WORKERS BY TOP TEN SOURCE COUNTRIES (PRINCIPAL APPLICANTS AND DEPENDANTS)

COUNTRY	1999			2000			2001		
	#	%	Rank	#	%	Rank	#	%	Rank
China, People's Republic of	21,290	22.99	1	27,410	23.12	1	28,816	21.02	1
India	6,903	7.46	2	12,403	10.46	2	13,649	9.95	2
Pakistan	5,013	5.42	3	9,921	8.37	3	9,012	6.57	3
Philippines	2,190	2.37	12	4,010	3.38	5	6,980	5.09	4
Korea, Republic of	3,901	4.22	4	4,342	3.66	4	6,854	5.00	5
Romania	2,527	2.73	9	3,387	2.86	7	4,409	3.22	6
United Arab Emirates	1,429	1.55	16	2,607	2.20	9	3,964	2.89	7
France	3,230	3.49	5	3,588	3.03	6	3,691	2.69	8
United Kingdom	2,526	2.73	10	2,786	2.35	8	3,265	2.38	9
Morocco	1,156	1.28	19	1,992	1.68	15	3,221	2.35	10
Russia	2,748	2.97	8	2,268	1.91	11	2,546	1.86	12
Iran	3,091	3.34	6	2,551	2.15	10	2,527	1.84	13
Taiwan	2,914	3.15	7	1,874	1.58	16	1,492	1.09	20
Total for Top Ten Only	**54,113**	**58.50**		**73,005**	**61.56**		**83,662**	**61.16**	
Total Other Countries	**38,365**	**41.50**		**45,536**	**38.42**		**53,257**	**38.84**	
Total	**92,478**	**100**		**118,541**	**100**		**137,119**	**100**	

source: http://www.cic.gc.ca/english/pdf/pub/facts2001.pdf

IMMIGRATION BY TOP TEN SOURCE COUNTRIES (PRINCIPAL APPLICANTS AND DEPENDANTS)

COUNTRY	1999			2000			2001		
	#	%	Rank	#	%	Rank	#	%	Rank
China, People's Republic of	29,112	15.33	1	36,715	16.15	1	40,295	16.10	1
India	17,429	9.18	2	26,086	11.48	2	27,812	11.11	2
Pakistan	9,295	4.89	3	14,182	6.24	3	15,339	6.13	3
Philippines	9,170	4.83	4	10,086	4.44	4	12,903	5.15	4
Korea, Republic of	7,216	3.80	5	7,626	3.35	5	9,604	3.84	5
United States	5,528	2.91	7	5,814	2.56	7	5,894	2.35	6
Iran	5,907	3.11	6	5,608	2.47	8	5,736	2.29	7
Romania	3,461	1.82	14	4,425	1.95	11	5,585	2.23	8
Sri Lanka	4,723	2.49	9	5,841	2.57	6	5,514	2.20	9
United Kingdom	4,478	2.36	10	4,647	2.04	10	5,345	2.14	10
Taiwan	5,464	2.88	8	3,511	1.54	14	3,111	1.24	19
Yugoslavia	1,490	0.78	29	4,723	2.08	9	2,786	1.11	22
Total for Top Ten Only	**98,322**	**51.78**		**121,328**	**53.38**		**134,028**	**53.54**	
Total Other Countries	**91,600**	**48.22**		**105,985**	**46.62**		**116,318**	**46.46**	
Total	**189,922**	**100**		**227,313**	**100**		**250,346**	**100**	

source: http://www.cic.gc.ca/english/pdf/pub/facts2001.pdf

Who Are Skilled Workers

Skilled workers are people whose education and work experience will help them find work and make a home for themselves as permanent residents in Canada. Applying to come to Canada as a Skilled Worker is not difficult. You will find all the information and forms you need to make your application here. **http://www.cic.gc.ca/english/applications/index.html.**

Refer to www.cic.gc.ca often. The rules for applying as a Skilled Worker can change. Before you apply, make sure your application follows the current rules. After you apply, check back for information about the steps that follow. You can also check the status of your application through this website. **http://www.cic.gc.ca/english/e-services/index.html**

Will You Qualify as a Skilled Worker?

Skilled workers are people who may become permanent residents because they are able to become economically established in Canada.

To be accepted as a Skilled Worker, applicants must:

- meet the minimum work experience requirements;
- prove that they have the funds required for settlement; and
- earn enough points in the six selection factors to meet the pass mark.

The following categories will help you determine if you can apply as Skilled Worker. You can assess your chances of being accepted. Consult each of the following areas for the current regulations regarding:

Minimum Work Experience Requirements

Skilled workers are people who may become permanent residents because they have the ability to become economically established in Canada.

You must meet the following minimum work experience requirements to allow you to apply as a skilled worker:

- You must have at least one year of full-time work experience. You must have been paid for this work.

- Your work experience must be in the category of **Skill Type 0**, or **Skill Level A or B** on the Canadian National Occupational Classification (NOC). (See below for instructions.)

- You must have had this experience within the last 10 years.

What are Skill Types

Skill Type 0 : These are the management occupations. All kinds of managers in their field of expertise fall under type 0.

Skill Level A: These are the occupations that required **university degree** at the bachelor's or master's or doctorate level for example Engineers, Physicians, Lawyers, Teachers.

Skill Level B: These are the occupations that requires college education or apprenticeship training for example 2 or 3 years diploma in the field of engineering / information technology or management sciences. Their designations may vary as Associate Engineer, Technologist and Technicians

- To know more about **Skill Type 0** or **Skill Level A or B,** visit this link **http://cnp2001noc.worklogic.com/e/matrix.pdf**

National Occupation Classification (NOC)

The NOC is a classification system for jobs in the Canadian economy. It describes duties, skills, talents and work settings for occupations.

National Occupation
Classification List

The following occupations are listed in Skill Type 0, Skill Level A or B of the National Occupation Classification List.

Code	A
0632	Accommodation Service Managers
5135	Actors and Comedians
1221	Administrative Officers
0114	Administrative Services Managers (other)
0312	Administrators - Post-Secondary Education and Vocational
2146	Aerospace Engineers
2222	Agricultural and Fish Products Inspectors
8252	Agricultural and Related Service Contractors and Managers
2123	Agricultural Representatives, Consultants and Specialists
2271	Air Pilots, Flight Engineers and Flying Instructors
2272	Air Traffic Control and Related Occupations
2244	Aircraft Instrument, Electrical and Avionics Mechanics, Technicians and Inspectors
7315	Aircraft Mechanics and Aircraft Inspectors
3234	Ambulance Attendants and Other Paramedical Occupations
5231	Announcers and Other Broadcasters
8257	Aquaculture Operators and Managers
2151	Architects
2251	Architectural Technologists and Technicians
0212	Architecture and Science Managers

5113	Archivists
5244	Artisans and Craftpersons
1235	Assessors, Valuators and Appraisers
5251	Athletes
5225	Audio and Video Recording Technicians
3141	Audiologists and Speech-Language Pathologists
5121	Authors and Writers
7321	Automotive Service Technicians, Truck Mechanics and Mechanical Repairers
Code	**B**
6252	Bakers
0122	Banking, Credit and Other Investment Managers
2221	Biological Technologists and Technicians
2121	Biologists and Related Scientists
7266	Blacksmiths and Die Setters
7262	Boilermakers
1231	Bookkeepers
7281	Bricklayers
5224	Broadcast Technicians
4163	Business Development Officers and Marketing Researchers and Consultants
0123	Business Services Managers (other)
6251	Butchers and Meat Cutters - Retail and Wholesale
Code	**C**
7272	Cabinetmakers
7247	Cable Television Service and Maintenance Technicians

3217	Cardiology Technologists
7271	Carpenters
9231	Central Control and Process Operators, Mineral and Metal Processing
6241	Chefs
2134	Chemical Engineers
2211	Chemical Technologists and Technicians
2112	Chemists
3122	Chiropractors
2231	Civil Engineering Technologists and Technicians
2131	Civil Engineers
6215	Cleaning Supervisors
5252	Coaches
4131	College and Other Vocational Instructors
7382	Commercial Divers
0643	Commissioned Officers, Armed Forces
0641	Commissioned Police Officers
4212	Community and Social Service Workers
0213	Computer and Information Systems Managers
2281	Computer and Network Operators and Web Technicians
2147	Computer Engineers (Except Software Engineers)
2174	Computer Programmers and Interactive Media Developers
7282	Concrete Finishers
5132	Conductors, Composers and Arrangers
1226	Conference and Event Planners

2224	Conservation and Fishery Officers
5112	Conservators and Curators
2234	Construction Estimators
2264	Construction Inspectors
0711	Construction Managers
7311	Construction Millwrights and Industrial Mechanics (Except Textile)
7215	Contractors and Supervisors, Carpentry Trades
7212	Contractors and Supervisors, Electrical Trades and Telecommunications
7217	Contractors and Supervisors, Heavy Construction Equipment Crews
7216	Contractors and Supervisors, Mechanic Trades
7214	Contractors and Supervisors, Metal Forming, Shaping and Erecting Trades
7219	Contractors and Supervisors, Other Construction Trades, Installers, Repairers
7213	Contractors and Supervisors, Pipefitting Trades
6242	Cooks
1227	Court Officers and Justices of the Peace
1244	Court Recorders and Medical Transcriptionists
7371	Crane Operators
1236	Customs, Ship and Other Brokers
Code	**D**
5134	Dancers
2172	Database Analysts and Data Administrators
2273	Deck Officers, Water Transport
3222	Dental Hygienists and Dental Therapists
3223	Dental Technologists, Technicians and Laboratory

3113	Dentists
3221	Denturists
3132	Dietitians and Nutritionists
2253	Drafting Technologists and Technicians
7372	Drillers and Blasters D Surface Mining, Quarrying and Construction
6214	Dry Cleaning and Laundry Supervisors
Code	**E**
4214	Early Childhood Educators and Assistants
4162	Economists and Economic Policy Researchers and Analysts
5122	Editors
4166	Education Policy Researchers, Consultants and Program Officers
4143	Educational Counsellors
7332	Electric Appliance Servicers and Repairers
2241	Electrical and Electronics Engineering Technologists and Technicians
2133	Electrical and Electronics Engineers
7333	Electrical Mechanics
7244	Electrical Power Line and Cable Workers
7241	Electricians (Except Industrial and Power System)
3218	Electroencephalographic and Other Diagnostic Technologists, n.e.c.
2242	Electronic Service Technicians (Household and Business
7318	Elevator Constructors and Mechanics
4213	Employment Counsellors
2274	Engineer Officers, Water Transport
2262	Engineering Inspectors and Regulatory Officers

0211	Engineering Managers
1222	Executive Assistants
6213	Executive Housekeepers
Code	**F**
0721	Facility Operation and Maintenance Managers
4153	Family, Marriage and Other Related Counsellors
8253	Farm Supervisors and Specialized Livestock Workers
8251	Farmers and Farm Managers
5222	Film and Video Camera Operators
1112	Financial and Investment Analysts
1111	Financial Auditors and Accountants
0111	Financial Managers
1114	Financial Officers (other)
0642	Fire Chiefs and Senior Firefighting Officers
6262	Firefighters
8261	Fishing Masters and Officers
8262	Fishing Vessel Skippers and Fishermen/women
7295	Floor Covering Installers
6212	Food Service Supervisors
2122	Forestry Professionals
2223	Forestry Technologists and Technicians
6272	Funeral Directors and Embalmers
Code	**G**
7253	Gas Fitters

2212	Geological and Mineral Technologists and Technicians
2144	Geological Engineers
2113	Geologists, Geochemists and Geophysicists
7292	Glaziers
0412	Government Managers - Economic Analysis, Policy Development
0413	Government Managers - Education Policy Development and Program Administration
0411	Government Managers - Health and Social Policy Development and Program Administration
6234	Grain Elevator Operators
5223	Graphic Arts Technicians
5241	Graphic Designers and Illustrators
Code	**H**
6271	Hairstylists and Barbers
3151	Head Nurses and Supervisors
3123	Health Diagnosing and Treating (Other Professional Occupations)
4165	Health Policy Researchers, Consultants and Program Officers
7312	Heavy-Duty Equipment Mechanics
0112	Human Resources Managers
Code	**I**
1228	Immigration, Employment Insurance and Revenue Officers
2141	Industrial and Manufacturing Engineers
2252	Industrial Designers
7242	Industrial Electricians
2233	Industrial Engineering and Manufacturing Technologists and Technicians
2243	Industrial Instrument Technicians and Mechanics

Code	
2171	Information Systems Analysts and Consultants
2263	Inspectors in Public and Environmental Health and Occupational Health and Safety
4216	Instructors (other)
4215	Instructors and Teachers of Persons with Disabilities
7293	Insulators
1233	Insurance Adjusters and Claims Examiners
6231	Insurance Agents and Brokers
1234	Insurance Underwriters
0121	Insurance, Real Estate and Financial Brokerage Managers
5242	Interior Designers
7264	Ironworkers
Code	**J**
7344	Jewellers, Watch Repairers and Related Occupations
5123	Journalists
4111	Judges
1227	Justices of the Peace
Code	**L**
2254	Land Survey Technologists and Technicians
2154	Land Surveyors
2225	Landscape and Horticultural Technicians and Specialists
2152	Landscape Architects
8255	Landscaping and Grounds Maintenance Contractors and Managers
4112	Lawyers and Quebec Notaries
1242	Legal Secretaries

0011	Legislators
5111	Librarians
5211	Library and Archive Technicians and Assistants
0511	Library, Archive, Museum and Art Gallery Managers
3233	Licensed Practical Nurses
1232	Loan Officers
8241	Logging Machinery Operators
Code	**M**
7316	Machine Fitters
7231	Machinists and Machining and Tooling Inspectors
0512	Managers - Publishing, Motion Pictures, Broadcasting and Performing Arts
0311	Managers in Health Care
0414	Managers in Public Administration (other)
0314	Managers in Social, Community and Correctional Services
0911	Manufacturing Managers
2255	Mapping and Related Technologists and Technicians
2161	Mathematicians, Statisticians and Actuaries
2232	Mechanical Engineering Technologists and Technicians
2132	Mechanical Engineers
3212	Medical Laboratory Technicians
3211	Medical Laboratory Technologists and Pathologists' Assistants
3215	Medical Radiation Technologists
1243	Medical Secretaries
3216	Medical Sonographers

3219	Medical Technologists and Technicians (other - except Dental Health)
2142	Metallurgical and Materials Engineers
2213	Meteorological Technicians
2114	Meteorologists
3232	Midwives and Practitioners of Natural Healing
2143	Mining Engineers
4154	Ministers of Religion
5226	Motion Pictures, Broadcasting (other Technical and Co-ordinating Occupations)
7322	Motor Vehicle Body Repairers
7334	Motorcycle and Other Related Mechanics
5212	Museums and Art Galleries (related Technical Occupations)
5133	Musicians and Singers
Code	N
4161	Natural and Applied Science Policy Researchers, Consultants and Program Officers
2261	Nondestructive Testers and Inspectors
8254	Nursery and Greenhouse Operators and Managers
Code	O
3143	Occupational Therapists
8232	Oil and Gas Well Drillers, Servicers, Testers and Related Workers
7331	Oil and Solid Fuel Heating Mechanics
3231	Opticians
3121	Optometrists
Code	P
7294	Painters and Decorators

5136	Painters, Sculptors and Other Visual Artists
9234	Papermaking and Coating Control Operators
4211	Paralegal and Related Occupations
5245	Patternmakers - Textile, Leather and Fur Products
5232	Performers (other)
1223	Personnel and Recruitment Officers
2145	Petroleum Engineers
9232	Petroleum, Gas and Chemical Process Operators
3131	Pharmacists
5221	Photographers
2115	Physical Sciences (Other Professional Occupations)
3112	Physicians - General Practitioners and Family Physicians
3111	Physicians - Specialist
2111	Physicists and Astronomers
3142	Physiotherapists
7252	Pipefitters
7284	Plasterers, Drywall Installers and Finishers and Lathers
7251	Plumbers
6261	Police Officers (Except Commissioned)
0132	Postal and Courier Services Managers
4122	Post-Secondary Teaching and Research Assistants
7243	Power System Electricians
7352	Power Systems and Power Station Operators
0811	Primary Production Managers (Except Agriculture)

7381	Printing Press Operators
4155	Probation and Parole Officers and Related Occupations
5131	Producers, Directors, Choreographers and Related Occupations
2148	Professional Engineers, n.e.c. (other)
1122	Professional Occupations in Business Services to Management
5124	Professional Occupations in Public Relations and Communications
4121	Professors - University
5254	Program Leaders and Instructors in Recreation and Sport
4168	Program Officers Unique to Government
1224	Property Administrators
4151	Psychologists
9233	Pulping Control Operators
1225	Purchasing Agents and Officers
0113	Purchasing Managers
Code	**R**
7361	Railway and Yard Locomotive Engineers
7314	Railway Carmen/women
7362	Railway Conductors and Brakemen/women
2275	Railway Traffic Controllers and Marine Traffic Regulators
6232	Real Estate Agents and Salespersons
0513	Recreation and Sports Program and Service Directors
4167	Recreation, Sports and Fitness Program Supervisors Consultants
7313	Refrigeration and Air Conditioning Mechanics
3152	Registered Nurses

4217	Religious Occupations (other)
0712	Residential Home Builders and Renovators
3214	Respiratory Therapists, Clinical Perfusionists and Cardio-Pulmonary Technologists
0631	Restaurant and Food Service Managers
6233	Retail and Wholesale Buyers
0621	Retail Trade Managers
6211	Retail Trade Supervisors
7291	Roofers and Shinglers
Code	
0611	Sales, Marketing and Advertising Managers
0313	School Principals and Administrators of Elementary and Secondary
1241	Secretaries (Except Legal and Medical)
1113	Securities Agents, Investment Dealers and Brokers
0012	Senior Government Managers and Officials
0013	Senior Managers - Financial, Communications and Other Business
0016	Senior Managers - Goods Production, Utilities, Transportation and Construction
0014	Senior Managers - Health, Education, Social and Community
0015	Senior Managers - Trade, Broadcasting and Other Services, n.e.c.
6216	Service Supervisors (other)
0651	Services Managers (other)
7261	Sheet Metal Workers
7343	Shoe Repairers and Shoemakers
7335	Small Engine and Equipment Mechanics (other)
4164	Social Policy Researchers, Consultants and Program Officers

4169	Social Science, n.e.c. (Other Professional Occupations)
4152	Social Workers
2173	Software Engineers
1121	Specialists in Human Resources
5253	Sports Officials and Referees
7252	Sprinkler System Installers
7351	Stationary Engineers and Auxiliary Equipment Operators
7252	Steamfitters, Pipefitters and Sprinkler System Installers
7263	Structural Metal and Platework Fabricators and Fitters
9223	Supervisors, Electrical Products Manufacturing
9222	Supervisors, Electronics Manufacturing
9225	Supervisors, Fabric, Fur and Leather Products Manufacturing
1212	Supervisors, Finance and Insurance Clerks
9213	Supervisors, Food, Beverage and Tobacco Processing
9215	Supervisors, Forest Products Processing
9224	Supervisors, Furniture and Fixtures Manufacturing
1211	Supervisors, General Office and Administrative Support Clerks
8256	Supervisors, Landscape and Horticulture
1213	Supervisors, Library, Correspondence and Related Information Clerks
8211	Supervisors, Logging and Forestry
7211	Supervisors, Machinists and Related Occupations
1214	Supervisors, Mail and Message Distribution Occupations
9211	Supervisors, Mineral and Metal Processing
8221	Supervisors, Mining and Quarrying

7222	Supervisors, Motor Transport and Other Ground Transit Operators
9221	Supervisors, Motor Vehicle Assembling
8222	Supervisors, Oil and Gas Drilling and Service
9226	Supervisors, Other Mechanical and Metal Products Manufacturing
9227	Supervisors, Other Products Manufacturing and Assembly
9212	Supervisors, Petroleum, Gas and Chemical Processing and Utilities
9214	Supervisors, Plastic and Rubber Products Manufacturing
7218	Supervisors, Printing and Related Occupations
7221	Supervisors, Railway Transport Operations
1215	Supervisors, Recording, Distributing and Scheduling Occupations
9216	Supervisors, Textile Processing
5227	Support Occupations in Motion Pictures, Broadcasting and the Performing Arts
2283	Systems Testing Technicians
Code	**T**
7342	Tailors, Dressmakers, Furriers and Milliners
4142	Teachers - Elementary School and Kindergarten
4141	Teachers - Secondary School
6221	Technical Sales Specialists - Wholesale Trade
0131	Telecommunication Carriers Managers
7246	Telecommunications Installation and Repair Workers
7245	Telecommunications Line and Cable Workers
7317	Textile Machinery Mechanics and Repairers
5243	Theatre, Fashion, Exhibit and Other Creative Designers
3144	Therapy and Assessment (Other Professional Occupations)

Code	
3235	Therapy and Assessment (other Technical Occupations)
7283	Tilesetters
7232	Tool and Die Makers
7383	Trades and Related Occupations (other)
5125	Translators, Terminologists and Interpreters
0713	Transportation Managers
Code	
8231	Underground Production and Development Miners
7341	Upholsterers
2153	Urban and Land Use Planners
2282	User Support Technicians
0912	Utilities Managers
Code	**V**
3114	Veterinarians
3213	Veterinary and Animal Health Technologists and
Code	**W**
7373	Water Well Drillers
2175	Web Designers and Developers
7265	Welders and Related Machine Operators

Determine Your NOC Category

Follow these steps to see if your work experience meets the requirements to apply as a skilled worker.

1. Find the title of any full-time jobs you had in the past 10 years using above National Occupation Classification list. This is a list of all jobs that are in Skill Type 0, Skill Level A or B on the NOC. **Write down the four-digit code located to the left of your job's title.**

2. Go to the NOC Web site: (*http://cnp2001noc.worklogic.com/e/welcome.shtml*) and type your four-digit job-code in the "Quick Search" box. Make sure you press the "GO" button. A description of your occupation will appear. Make sure the description and "Main Duties" describe what you did at your last jobs.

Note: you do **not** have to meet the "Employment Requirements" listed in the description.

If the initial description and list of main duties **matches** what you did at your last jobs, you can count this experience as when you apply as a skilled worker. You can also earn points in Factor 3 of the Selection Factors.

If the description **does not match** your work experience then you might not have the experience you need to apply as a skilled worker. Look through the NOC list to see if another occupation matches your experience. Check all of the jobs you had in the past 10 years to see if you have at least one year of work experience in a job that will qualify you as a skilled worker.

Check the list of restricted occupations. If your work experience is in a restricted occupation then you **cannot** use it to qualify for the Skilled Worker category.

What are restricted occupations: To protect the Canadian labour market Citizenship and Immigration Canada has to make sure that Canada does not have too many people with the same skills.

There are no restricted occupations at the time of this publication

You do not meet the minimum requirements if:

- none of your work experience is listed in the NOC list;
- your experience did **not** occur in the 10 years before you applied; or

- your only work experience is in a restricted occupation.

If you do not meet the minimum work experience requirements, your application as a Skilled Worker will be refused.

Few examples of NOC Listed professions

6271   Hairstylists and Barbers

Hairstylists and barbers cut and style hair and perform related services. They are employed in hairstyling or hairdressing salons, barber shops, vocational schools, health care establishments and theatre, film and television establishments.

Example Titles

barber
barber apprentice
hair colour technician
hairdresser
hairdresser apprentice
hairstylist
hairstylist apprentice
wig stylist

Main duties

Hairstylists perform some or all of the following duties:

- Suggest hair style compatible with client's physical features or determine style from client's instructions and preferences
- Cut, trim, taper, curl, wave, perm and style hair
- Apply bleach, tints, dyes or rinses to colour, frost or streak hair
- Analyze hair and scalp condition and provide basic treatment or advice on beauty care treatments for scalp and hair
- May shampoo and rinse hair
- May train or supervise other hairstylists, hairstylist apprentices and helpers.

Barbers perform some or all of the following duties:

- Cut and trim hair according to client's instructions or preferences

- Shave and trim beards and moustaches

- May shampoo hair and provide other hair treatment, such as waving, straightening and tinting and may also provide scalp conditioning massages

- May train and supervise other barbers and barber apprentices.

Employment requirements for Hair Stylists

Some secondary school education is required.

- Completion of a two- or three-year hairstyling apprenticeship program or completion of a college or other program in hairstyling combined with on-the-job training is usually required.

- Several years of experience may replace formal education and training.

- Employers may require applicants to provide a hairstyling demonstration before being hired.

- There are various provincial/territorial certification and licensing requirements for hairstylists, ranging from trade certification to licensing by a provincial/territorial association. Interprovincial trade certification (Red Seal) is also available for qualified hairstylists. Barbers

- Some secondary school education is required.

- Completion of a two-year apprenticeship or other barber program is usually required.

- On-the-job training may be substituted for formal education.

- There are various provincial/territorial certification and licensing requirements for barbers, ranging from trade certification to licensing by a provincial/territorial association. Barbers can also obtain interprovincial trade certification (Red Seal) as qualified hairstylists.

Additional information

- Red Seal trade certification allows for interprovincial mobility.

2232   Mechanical Engineering Technologists and Technicians

Mechanical engineering technologists and technicians provide technical support and services or may work independently in mechanical engineering fields such as the design, development, maintenance and testing of machines, components, tools, heating and ventilating systems, power generation and power conversion plants, manufacturing plants and equipment. They are employed by consulting engineering, manufacturing and processing companies, institutions and government departments.

Example Titles

aeronautical technologist
heating designer
HVAC (heating, ventilating & air conditioning) technologist
machine designer
marine engineering technologist mechanical engineering technician
mechanical engineering technologist
mechanical technologist
mould designer
thermal station technician
tool and die designer
tool designer

Main duties

Mechanical engineering technologists perform some or all of the following duties:

- Prepare and interpret conventional and computer-assisted design (CAD) engineering designs, drawings, and specifications for machines and components, power transmission systems, process piping, heating, ventilating and air-conditioning systems

- Prepare cost and material estimates, project schedules and reports

- Conduct tests and analyses of machines, components and materials to determine their performance, strength, response to stress and other characteristics

- Design moulds, tools, dies, jigs and fixtures for use in manufacturing processes

- Inspect mechanical installations and construction

- Prepare contract and tender documents

- Supervise, monitor and inspect mechanical installations and construction projects
- Prepare standards and schedules and supervise mechanical maintenance programs or operations of mechanical plants.

Mechanical engineering technicians perform some or all of the following duties:

- Assist in preparing conventional and computer assisted design (CAD) engineering designs, drawings and specifications
- Carry out a limited range of mechanical tests and analyses of machines, components and materials
- Assist in the design of moulds, tools, dies, jigs and fixtures for use in manufacturing processes
- Assist in inspection of mechanical installations and construction projects
- Participate in the installation, repair and maintenance of machinery and equipment.

Employment requirements

- Completion of a two- or three-year college program in mechanical engineering technology is usually required for mechanical engineering technologists.
- Completion of a one- or two-year college program in mechanical engineering technology is usually required for mechanical engineering technicians.
- Certification in mechanical engineering technology or in a related field is available through provincial associations of engineering/applied science technologists and technicians and may be required for some positions.
- A period of supervised work experience, usually two years, is required before certification.
- In Quebec, membership in the regulatory body is required to use the title of Professional Technologist.

Additional information

- There is mobility to other related occupations such as technical sales or drafting technologists and technicians.
- Progression to supervisory occupations such as mechanical construction supervisor, manufacturing supervisor or operations maintenance manager is possible with experience.

2133   Electrical and Electronics Engineers

Electrical and electronics engineers design, plan, research, evaluate and test electrical and electronic equipment and systems. They are employed by electrical utilities, communications companies, manufacturers of electrical and electronic equipment, consulting firms, and by a wide range of manufacturing, processing and transportation industries and government.

Example Titles

avionics engineer
control systems engineer
design engineer, electrical
distribution planning engineer, electrical engineer
electrical network engineer
electronics engineer
instrumentation and control engineer
planning engineer, electrical systems
process control engineer, electrical
roadway lighting design engineer
television systems engineer
test engineer, electronics

Main duties

Electrical and electronics engineers perform some or all of the following duties:

- Conduct research into the feasibility, design, operation and performance of electrical generation and distribution networks, electrical machinery and components and electronic communications, instrumentation and control systems, equipment, and components
- Prepare material cost and timing estimates, reports and design specifications for electrical and electronic systems and equipment
- Design electrical and electronic circuits, components, systems and equipment
- Supervise and inspect the installation, modification, testing and operation of electrical and electronic systems and equipment
- Develop maintenance and operating standards for electrical and electronic systems and equipment
- Investigate electrical or electronic failures

- Prepare contract documents and evaluate tenders for construction or maintenance

- Supervise technicians, technologists, programmers, analysts and other engineers.

Electrical and electronics engineers may specialize in a number of areas including electrical design for residential, commercial or industrial installations, electrical power generation and transmission, and instrumentation and control systems.

Employment requirements

- A bachelor's degree in electrical or electronics engineering or in an appropriate related engineering discipline is required.

- A master's or doctoral degree in a related engineering discipline may be required.

- Licensing by a provincial or territorial association of professional engineers is required to approve engineering drawings and reports and to practise as a Professional Engineer (P.Eng.).

- Engineers are eligible for registration following graduation from an accredited educational program, and after three or four years of supervised work experience in engineering and passing a professional practice examination.

- Supervisory and senior positions in this unit group require experience.

Selection Factors

Work Experience (maximum 21 points)

You will be awarded selection points for the number of years you spent in full-time, paid work. Your jobs must be listed in the Skill type 0 or Skill Levels A or B in the National Occupation Classification.

Years of experience	1	2	3	4+
Points	15	17	19	21

Proof of Funds

The Government of Canada does not provide financial support to new skilled worker immigrants.

You **must** show that you have enough money to support yourself and your dependants after you arrive in Canada. You cannot borrow this money from another person. You must be able to use this money to support your family.

You will need to provide proof of your funds when you submit your application for immigration. The amount of money that you need to have to support your family is determined by the size of your family.

Number of Family Members	Funds Required (in Canadian dollars)
1	$9,186
2	$11,482
3	$14,280
4	$17,286
5	$19,323
6	$21,360
7 or more	$23,397

You do **not** have to show that you have these funds if you have arranged employment in Canada.

How Much Money Should you Bring?

Find out how much it costs to live where you are planning to settle in Canada.

- Bring as much money as possible to make moving and finding a home in Canada easier.
- This website can provide you valuable information about living cost in Ontario. **www.settlement.org**

Disclosure of funds:

If you are carrying more than CDN $10,000, tell a Canadian official when you arrive in Canada. **If you do not tell an official you may be fined or put in prison.** These funds could be in the form of:

- cash
- securities in bearer form (for example: stocks, bonds, debentures, treasury bills); or
- negotiable instruments in bearer form (for example: bankers' drafts, cheques, travellers' cheques, money orders.)

Language Proficiency

The ability to communicate and work in one or both of Canada's official languages is very important to you, as a skilled worker. Abilities in English, French or both will help you in the Canadian labour market.

Language proficiency is one of the six selection factors for skilled workers. You will be awarded up to 24 points for your basic, moderate or high abilities in English and French. You will be given points based on your ability to:

- listen;
- speak;
- read; and
- write.

Description of Each Level of Ability:

Use the following chart to assess your skill levels according to the Canadian Language Benchmarks. Follow the links for a description of each skill level.

Proficiency Level	Ability			
	Speaking	Listening	Reading	Writing
HIGH: You can communicate effectively in most social and work situations.	Speaking: High	Listening: High	Reading: High	Writing: High
MODERATE: you can communicate comfortably in familiar social and work situations.	Speaking: Moderate	Listening: Moderate	Reading: Moderate	Writing: Moderate
BASIC: You can communicate in predictable contexts and on familiar topics, but with some difficulty.	Speaking: Basic	Listening: Basic	Reading: Basic	Writing: Basic
NO: You do not meet the above criteria for basic proficiency.	Does not meet Basic Level.	Does not meet Basic Level.	Does not meet Basic Level.	Does not meet Basic Level.

Your First and Second Official Languages

If you have some abilities in both the English and French language, decide which language you are more comfortable using. This is your First Official Language. The other is your Second Official Language.

Canadian Language Benchmark 8

Speaking: High Level

Global Performance Descriptor

- Learner can communicate effectively in most daily practical and social situations, and in familiar routine work situations.
- Can participate in conversations with confidence.
- Can speak on familiar topics at both concrete and abstract levels (10 to 15 minutes).
- Can provide descriptions, opinions and explanations; can synthesize abstract complex ideas, can hypothesize.
- In social interaction, learner demonstrates increased ability to respond appropriately to the formality level of the situation.
- Can use a variety of sentence structures, including embedded and report structures, and an expanded inventory of concrete, idiomatic and conceptual language.
- Grammar and pronunciation errors rarely impede communication.
- Discourse is reasonably fluent.
- Uses phone on less familiar and some non-routine matters.

Performance Conditions

- Interaction is with one or more people, face to face or on the phone. It is often at a normal rate.
- Speech is partly predictable and does not always support the utterance.
- Considerable level of stress affects performance when verbal interaction may result in personal consequences (e.g. on the job).
- Audience is small familiar and unfamiliar informal groups.
- Setting and context are familiar, clear and predictable.
- Topic is familiar, concrete and abstract.
- Pictures and other visuals are used.
- Length of presentation is 15 to 20 minutes.

Interaction one-on-one

- Interaction is face to face or on the phone.
- Interaction is formal or semi-formal.
- Learner can partially prepare the exchange.

Interaction in a group

- Interaction takes place in a familiar group of up to 10 people.
- The topic or issue is familiar, non-personal, concrete and abstract.
- Interaction is informal or semi-formal.

Canadian Language Benchmark 8

Listening: High Level

Global Performance Descriptor

- Learner can comprehend main points, details, speaker's purpose, attitudes, levels of formality and styles in oral discourse in moderately demanding contexts.
- Can follow most formal and informal conversations, and some technical work-related discourse in own field at a normal rate of speech.
- Can follow discourse about abstract and complex ideas on a familiar topic.
- Can comprehend an expanded range of concrete, abstract and conceptual language.
- Can determine mood, attitudes and feelings.
- Can understand sufficient vocabulary, idioms and colloquial expressions to follow detailed stories of general popular interest.
- Can follow clear and coherent extended instructional texts and directions.
- Can follow clear and coherent phone messages on unfamiliar and non-routine matters.
- Often has difficulty following rapid, colloquial/idiomatic or regionally accented speech between native speakers.

Performance Conditions

- Tasks are in a standard format, with items to circle, match, fill in a blank, and complete a chart.
- Learner is adequately briefed for focused listening.
- Communication is face to face, observed live, or video- and audio-mediated (e.g., tape, TV, radio).
- Speech is clear at a normal rate.
- Instructions are clear and coherent.
- Listening texts are monologues/presentations and dialogues (five to 10 minutes), within familiar general topics and technical discourse in own field.
- Topics are familiar.
- Presentation/lecture is informal or semi-formal with the use of pictures, visuals (10 to 15 minutes).
- Learner is briefed for focused listening.
- Speech is clear, at a normal rate.

Canadian Language Benchmark 8

Reading: High Level

Global Performance Descriptor

- Learner can follow main ideas, key words and important details in an authentic two to three-page text on a familiar topic, but within an only partially predictable context.
- May read popular newspaper and magazine articles and popular easy fiction as well as academic and business materials.
- Can extract relevant points, but often requires clarification of idioms and of various cultural references.
- Can locate and integrate several specific pieces of information in visually complex texts (e.g., tables, directories) or across paragraphs or sections of text.
- Text can be on abstract, conceptual or technical topics, containing facts, attitudes and opinions. Inference may be required to identify the writer's bias and the purpose/function of text.

- Learner reads in English for information, to learn the language, to develop reading skills.
- Uses a unilingual dictionary when reading for precision vocabulary building.

Performance Conditions

- Text is one page, five to 10 paragraphs long and is related to personal experience or familiar context.
- Text is legible, easy to read; is in print or neat handwriting.
- Instructions are clear and explicit, but not always presented step by step.
- Pictures may accompany text.
- Context is relevant, but not always familiar and predictable.
- Text has clear organization.
- Text content is relevant (e.g., commercials/advertising features, business/form letters, brochures.)
- Informational text is eight to 15 paragraphs long with clear organization in print or electronic form.
- Pictures often accompany text.
- Language is both concrete and abstract, conceptual and technical.
- Text types: news articles, stories, short articles, reports, editorials, opinion essays.

Canadian Language Benchmark 8

Writing: High Level

Global Performance Descriptor

- Learner demonstrates fluent ability in performing moderately complex writing tasks.
- Can link sentences and paragraphs (three or four) to form coherent texts to express ideas on familiar abstract topics, with some support for main ideas, and with an appropriate sense of audience.
- Can write routine business letters (e.g., letters of inquiry, cover letters for applications) and personal and formal social messages.

- Can write down a set of simple instructions, based on clear oral communication or simple written procedural text of greater length.

- Can fill out complex formatted documents.

- Can extract key information and relevant detail from a page-long text and write an outline or a one-paragraph summary.

- Demonstrates good control over common sentence patterns, coordination and subordination, and spelling and mechanics. Has occasional difficulty with complex structures (e.g., those reflecting cause and reason, purpose, comment), naturalness of phrases and expressions, organization and style.

Performance Conditions

- Circumstances range from informal to more formal occasions.

- Addressees are familiar.

- Topics are of immediate everyday relevance.

- Text is one or two short paragraphs in length.

- Text to reproduce is one or two pages in legible handwriting or print, or may be a short oral text (10 to 15 minutes).

- Texts are varied and may be of a specialized or technical nature.

- Learner may fill out a teacher-prepared summary grid to aid note taking or summarizing.

- Forms have over 40 items/pieces of information.

- Messages are two or three paragraphs in length.

- Brief texts required in pre-set formats are one to several sentences up to one paragraph long.

- Learner text is three or four paragraphs long, on non-personal abstract but familiar topics and issues.

- Where necessary for the task, learners must include information presented to them from other sources (e.g., photographs, drawings, reference text/research information, diagrams).

Calculate Your Language Points

Use the descriptions from the table above to score your language abilities.

First Official Language (English)				
	Speaking	**Listening**	**Reading**	**Writing**
High proficiency	4	4	4	4
Moderate proficiency	2	2	2	2
Basic proficiency	1	1	1	1
Please Note: You can score a maximum of only two points in total for basic-level proficiency.				
No proficiency	0	0	0	0
Second Official Language (French)				
	Speaking	**Listening**	**Reading**	**Writing**
High proficiency	2	2	2	2
Moderate proficiency	2	2	2	2
Basic proficiency	1	1	1	1
Please Note: You can score a maximum of only two points in total for basic-level proficiency.				
No proficiency	0	0	0	0

Language ability documentation

If you are claiming language skills on your application, you **must** provide **conclusive proof** of your language skills. You must choose one of two options to do this. You can:

1. take an official language test by an approved organization; or
2. provide other written documentation that supports your claim.

Providing Other Written Evidence

If you choose **not** to take an approved language test, you must prove your ability to speak, listen, read and write Canada's official languages through other written evidence. You must provide written proof and explanation that **clearly** shows you meet the benchmark criteria listed in the Canadian Language Benchmarks in each of the four skills:

You Must: Submit your written explanation and documentation with your application. This material should include:

- a written submission explaining your training in English or French;
- an explanation of how you commonly use English or French;
- official documentation of education in English or French; and
- official documentation of work experience in English or French.

What Happens Next:

An officer from Citizenship and Immigration Canada will look at the evidence you include with your application.

- Your submission must satisfy the officer that your language skills meet the benchmarks for the level you are claiming.
- The officer does not have to ask you for more evidence so include as much evidence and documentation with your application as you can.
- The officer will not interview you to assess your language skills.
- The officer will award points for your language ability based on what you send with your application. You will not know how many points the CIC Officer gives you for your language skills or if the CIC Officer is satisfied that you have **clearly** demonstrated the level of language skills you claim on your application.

Note: We **strongly recommend** that you take an official language test if you are claiming skills in a language that you have not used from birth.

Official Language Testing

The best way to provide proof of language skills is to take a language proficiency test given by an organization approved by Citizenship and Immigration Canada (CIC). If you do so, you will be able to see exactly how many points you will receive for the language factor according to your test results.

You Must:

- Make arrangements for testing by an approved organization. You will have to pay the costs.
- Include the results of your test with your immigration application.

What Happens Next:

- You can use the equivalency charts to see exactly how many points you will earn based on your test results.
- The test results will be used by CIC as conclusive proof of your language skills.
- You can use language test results for one year from the time you took the test.

Approved Language Tests

You can arrange to take a language test from any of the following approved organizations:

English Tests

- International English Language Testing System (IELTS)
  http://www.ielts.org/
- Canadian International Language Proficiency Index Program (CELPIP)

French Tests

- Test d'Evaluation de Francais (TEF)

Equivalency Charts

Once you have taken a language test from an approved organization, you can see how many points you will earn:

1. If you took an **International English Language Testing System (IELTS)** test;

2. If you took the **Canadian English Language Proficiency Index Program (CELPIP)**; http://www.ares.ubc.ca/CELPIP/index.html or

3. If you took a **Test d'Evaluation de Francais**. http://www.fda.ccip.fr/sinformer/tef/eng_default.htm

Test Score Equivalency Chart: International English Language Testing System

Level	Points (per ability)	Test Results for each Ability			
		Speaking	Listening	Reading	Writing
High (CLB/SLC 8-12)	First Official Language: **4**	7.0 - 9.0	7.0 - 9.0	7.0 - 9.0	7.0 - 9.0
	Second Official Language: **2**				
Moderate (CLB/SLC 6-7)	**2**	5.0 - 6.9	5.0 - 6.9	5.0 - 6.9	5.0 - 6.9
Basic (CLB/SLC 4-5)	**1** (to a maximum of 2)	4.0 - 4.9	4.0 - 4.9	4.0 - 4.9	4.0 - 4.9
No (CLB/SLC 0-3)	**0**	Less than 4.0	Less than 4.0	Less than 4.0	Less than 4.0

Test Score Equivalency Chart: Canadian English Language Proficiency Index Program

Level	Points (per ability)	Test Results for each Ability			
		Speaking	Listening	Reading	Writing
High (CLB/SLC 8-12)	First Official Language: **4**	4H	4H	4H	4H
	Second Official Language: **2**	5	5	5	5
		6	6	6	6
Moderate (CLB/SLC 6-7)	**2**	3H	3H	3H	3H
		4L	4L	4L	4L
Basic (CLB/SLC 4-5)	**1** (to a max. of 2)	2H	2H	2H	2H
		3L	3L	3L	3L
No (CLB/SLC 0-3)	**0**	0	0	0	0
		1	1	1	1
		2L	2L	2L	2L

Test Score Equivalency Chart: Test d'Evaluation de Francais

Level	Points (per ability)	Test Results for each Ability			
		Speaking	Listening	Reading	Writing
High	First Official Language: **4**	Level 5	Level 5	Level 5	Level 5
(CLB/SLC 8-12)	Second Official Language: 2	Level 6	Level 6 (271-360 points)	Level 6 (226-300 points)	Level 6
Moderate (CLB/SLC 6-7)	**2**	Level 4	Level 4 (199-270 points)	Level 4 (166-225 points)	Level 4
Basic (CLB/SLC 4-5)	**1** (to a maximum of 2)	Level 3	Level 3 (163-198 points)	Level 3 (136-165 points)	Level 3
No (CLB/SLC 0-3)	**0**	Level 0 Level 1 Level 2	Level 0 Level 1 Level 2 (0-162 points)	Level 0 Level 1 Level 2 (0-135 points)	Level 0 Level 1 Level

Six Selection Factors and Pass Mark

These charts show how points are awarded in the six selection factors.

Factor One: Education	Maximum 25
You have a Master's Degree or Ph.D. **and** at least 17 years of full-time or full-time equivalent study.	25
You have two or more university degrees at the bachelor's level **and** at least 15 years of full-time or full-time equivalent study.	22
You have a three-year diploma, trade certificate or apprenticeship **and** at least 15 years of full-time or full-time equivalent study.	22
You have a two-year university degree at the bachelor's level **and** at least 14 years of full-time or full-time equivalent study.	20
You have a two-year diploma, trade certificate or apprenticeship **and** at least 14 years of full-time or full-time equivalent study.	20
You have a one-year university degree at the bachelor's level **and** at least 13 years of full-time or full-time equivalent study.	15
You have a one-year diploma, trade certificate or apprenticeship **and** at least 13 years of full-time or full-time equivalent study.	15
You have a one-year diploma, trade certificate or apprenticeship **and** at least 12 years of full-time or full-time equivalent study.	12
You completed high school.	5
Learn more about the specific requirements and definitions of terms.	
Factor Two: Official Languages	**Maximum 24**
1st Official Language	
High proficiency (per ability)	4
Moderate proficiency (per ability)	2
Basic proficiency (per ability)	1 to maximum of 2
No proficiency	0
Possible maximum (all 4 abilities)	16
2nd Official Language	
High proficiency (per ability)	2
Moderate proficiency (per ability)	2
Basic proficiency (per ability)	1 to maximum of

	2
No proficiency	0
Possible maximum (all 4 abilities)	8

Learn more about the specific requirements and the documents you need.

Factor Three: Experience	Maximum 21
1 year	15
2 years	17
3 years	19
4 years	21

Learn more about specific requirements for earning work experience points.

Factor Four: Age	Maximum 10
21 to 49 years at time of application	10

Less 2 points for each year over 49 or under 21

View the full age chart to determine your points.

Factor Five: Arranged Employment In Canada	Maximum 10
You have a Human Resources Development Canada (HRDC) confirmed offer of permanent employment.	10

You are applying from within Canada and have a temporary work permit that is:

HRDC confirmed, including sectoral confirmations; or	10
HRDC confirmation exempt under NAFTA, GATS, CCFTA, or significant economic benefit (i.e. intra-company transferee.)	10

Learn more about specific requirements and conditions. by visiting

http://www.cic.gc.ca/english/skilled/qual-5-4.html

	Maximum 10
Spouse's (wife) or common-law partner's education	3 – 5
Minimum one year full-time authorized work in Canada	5
Minimum two years full-time authorized post-secondary study in Canada	5
Have received points under the Arranged Employment in Canada factor	5
Family relationship in Canada	5

Learn more about specific requirements and conditions.

Total	Maximum 100
Pass Mark	75

Selection Criteria	Maximum Points
Education	25
Official languages (English and/or French)	24
Employment experience	21
Age	10
Arranged employment in Canada	10
Adaptability	10
TOTAL	100

Will You Qualify?

1. If your score is **the same or higher** than the pass mark, then you may qualify to immigrate to Canada as a skilled worker. **After reading and understanding** all information, if you wish to apply for immigration, consult the application instructions.

2. If your score is **less** than the pass mark, you are not likely to qualify to immigrate to Canada as a Skilled Worker. We recommend that you do not apply at this time.

3. You may submit a formal application if you believe that there are factors that would show that you are able to become economically established in Canada. Send a detailed letter with your application explaining why you think you are able to become economically established in Canada. Include any documents that support your claim.

Please note:

If you applied before **January 1, 2002** and have not received a selection decision by March 31, 2003, your application will be evaluated under the new criteria with a pass mark of 70.

If you applied **on or after January 1, 2002** and did not receive a selection decision by June 28, 2002 when the new rules came into effect, your application will be evaluated under the new criteria with a pass mark of 75.

Principal Applicant

If you are married or living with a common-law partner, you and your spouse or common-law partner must decide who will be the principal applicant. The other person will be considered the dependant in the applications.

Note: A common-law partner is the person who has lived with you in a conjugal relationship for at least one year. Common-law partner refers to **both opposite-sex and same-sex couples.**

Use the self-assessment test to help you determine which person would earn the most points. The person who would earn the most points should apply as the principal applicant.

Try the <u>on-line Self-Assessment</u> at this site http://www.cic.gc.ca/english/skilled/assess/index.html to see how many points you would earn in the six selection factors explained above.

Application Fees

There are two application fees you will have to pay when you apply to immigrate to Canada as a skilled worker:

1. Processing Fee:

- Pay this when you apply.
- This fee **is not** refundable.

2. Right of Permanent Residence Fee:

- You can pay this any time while Citizenship and Immigration Canada (CIC) is processing your application. You must pay this before CIC can issue you your permanent residence visa.
- This fee **is** refundable if:
- you cancelled your application;
- CIC did not issue your visa to you; or
- you did not use your visa.

FEE SCHEDULE

for Citizenship and Immigration Services

A number of cost recovery and administrative fees are payable by applicants for processing applications of various types and for certain citizenship and immigration procedures. However, all fees are subject to change without notice. In general, fees are payable at the time of application. Please check with your nearest Citizenship and Immigration Canada office or Canadian mission abroad for confirmation.

Note: All amounts are in Canadian dollars.

Fees For Applications To Remain In Canada As A Permanent Resident

Spouse or Common-law Partner in Canada Class	
Sponsorship application (per application)	$75
Principal applicant	$475
A family member of the principal applicant who is 22 years of age or older, or is less than 22 years of age and is a spouse or common-law partner	$550
A family member of the principal applicant who is less than 22 years of age and is not a spouse or common-law partner	$150
Note: Fees assessed under the Spouse or Common-law Partner in Canada Class are payable, along with the sponsorship fee, when the sponsor files the sponsorship application. Refunds will be issued only if the sponsor withdraws the sponsorship application before processing of the application has begun. The $75 sponsorship fee will not normally be refunded.	
Other applicants	
Principal applicant	$550
A family member of the principal applicant who is 22 years of age or older, or is less than 22 years of age and is a spouse or common-law partner	$550
A family member of the principal applicant who is less than 22 years of age and is not a spouse or common-law partner	$150
Permit Holders Class	
Applicant	$325
Application under Section 25 of the Act*	
Principal applicant	$550
A family member of the principal applicant who is 22 years of age or	$550

older, or is less than 22 years of age and is a spouse or common-law partner	
A family member of the principal applicant who is less than 22 years of age and is not a spouse or common-law partner	$150

*Under this section, the Minister of Citizenship and Immigration may grant permanent resident status to an inadmissible foreign national based on humanitarian and compassionate considerations or public policy considerations.

Note: Always check current fee structure by visiting following CIC website before filing your immigration application.

http://www.cic.gc.ca/english/applications/fees.html#swpf

Additional Fees:

You will have to pay the fees related to obtaining:

- your medical examination;
- police certificates; and
- language testing.

Medical Examinations

You must pass a medical examination before coming to Canada. Your dependants must also pass a medical examination even if they are not coming with you.

Applications for permanent residence will not be accepted if that person's health:

- is a danger to public health or safety;
- would cause excessive demand on health or social services in Canada; or
- would affect potential employability or productivity.

Medical Examination Instructions

Instructions on how to take the medical examination will normally be sent to you after you submit your application to the Visa Office.

Validity

You can only use your examination results in your application for 12 months from when you had the examination. If your visa is not processed in this time, you will have to take another examination.

Authorized Doctors

Your own doctor cannot do the medical examination. You must see a physician on Canada's list of <u>Designated Medical Practitioners</u> (DMP). with respect to each country on this link
http://www.cic.gc.ca/english/contacts/medical.html

Medical Report Procedures

Medical reports and x-rays for the medical examination become the property of the Canadian Immigration Medical Authorities and cannot be returned to you.

The doctor will not tell you the results of the medical examination. The doctor will let you know if you have a health-related problem.

The DMP does **not** make the final decision. Citizenship and Immigration Canada will make the final decision on whether or not your medical examination has been passed for immigration purposes.

The Visa Office will tell you in writing if there is a problem with your medical examination.

WHO MAY REPRESENT YOU

A representative may be a lawyer, a consultant or any other person including a friend, whom you hire for a fee or ask to help you do any of the following at no charge: (1) apply for permanent residence or a temporary stay in Canada; (2) submit a refugee claim; (3) appear in front of an adjudicator; (4) appeal a decision; (5) apply for citizenship; or (6) request information on matters dealing with the *Immigration Act* or the *Citizenship Act.*

What you should know before seeking the services of someone to help with your application

Do you need a representative?

- Citizenship and Immigration Canada (CIC**) does not require** you to have a representative. CIC have tried to make the application kits as simple as possible so that you can complete them yourself. You can get additional information on how to complete an application from the CIC Web site at **http://www.cic.gc.ca/english/contacts/call.html** or from a CIC Call Centre

- If you decide to use the services of a representative, you are free to do so.

- **CIC treats all applicants equally and does not provide preferential service to applicants with representatives.**

Who can act as a representative?

- Anyone can act as a representative.

- Only lawyers licensed to practise in Canada can represent you at the Federal Court.

- CIC can provide information on your file only to people who are either (1) Canadian citizens, (2) permanent residents of Canada or (3) physically present in Canada. Representatives who live outside Canada and are neither Canadian citizens nor permanent residents might be unable to help you.

- Volunteer and non-governmental organizations that deal with immigrants may provide free services.

General points

- CIC cannot recommend representatives or vouch for their honesty or skills. It is your responsibility to make sure that the representative you choose is ethical and competent to perform the services required. You should not be afraid to ask the representative (whether a lawyer or a consultant) for references or for other proof that he or she has the necessary skills.

- **Beware of representatives who claim that you will get a visa, obtain citizenship or benefit from special treatment from the Canadian government by using their services. CIC is not associated with any representatives.**

- Be cautious when dealing with foreign-based representatives. Such companies or individuals may be outside the reach of Canadian law, and there may be no protection or remedy available in Canada to a dissatisfied client.

Lawyers

- Lawyers practising in Canada are regulated by provincial regulatory bodies. Only a lawyer who is a member in good standing of a provincial or territorial law society may practise law. The law societies regulate lawyers and can investigate complaints against members, impose discipline and provide financial compensation to clients who are victims of negligence or misconduct.

- If you live in Canada and you want to hire a lawyer, call the law society of the province or territory in which you live for the names of lawyers. In many cases, you can consult a lawyer free of charge for half an hour before deciding if you want to hire him or her. However, in some cases, a fee may be charged for the consultation.

Immigration consultants

- Immigration consultants are not regulated by either the federal or provincial governments of Canada.

- Find out if the consultant (whether he or she is in Canada or overseas) belongs to a professional association in Canada and ask about his or her experience with immigration or citizenship matters.

- Call the Better Business Bureau (BBB) to find out if the consultant has a satisfactory rating. Business people who fail to respond to letters of complaint sent to the BBB receive an unsatisfactory rating.

Dealing with representatives

- CIC requires your written authorization in order to release information to your representative.

- You may give your own mailing address or the mailing address of your representative as a point of contact for CIC. If you choose to give your representative's address, all correspondence from CIC including notices for interviews, requests for information, medical forms and visas, will be sent to the representative.

- If you change representatives or stop using their services, you must cancel your authorization in writing to CIC or CIC will continue dealing with them. If you hire a new representative, you will have to provide a new authorization to CIC.

- Make sure that the representative who helps you with your application is willing to be identified as your representative.

Information given to CIC must be truthful

- Submitting false or misleading information to CIC can lead to the refusal of your application, the cancellation of your visa, the revocation of your citizenship, your deportation from Canada, and criminal charges being laid against you.

- You are responsible for any documents you submit to CIC or that your representative submits on your behalf.

Where to go for help if things go wrong

CIC cannot help you if you have a dispute with your representative as it is a private matter between the two of you. However, you may write to the CIC office dealing with your case or to the following address to inform CIC of the situation:

> Citizenship and Immigration Canada
> Social Policy and Programs
> Selection Branch
> Jean Edmonds Tower North, 7th Floor
> 300 Slater Street
> Ottawa, Ontario KIA 1L1

Note: You should file a complaint with the proper authorities as soon as possible if you encounter serious difficulties with your representative as limitation periods may apply.

If your representative is a lawyer practising in Canada

- Address your complaint to the law society of the province or territory where your lawyer practises. Law societies impose a code of conduct on their members to try to protect the public interest. They have rules for disciplining lawyers and compensating clients. You may be able to obtain financial compensation from the law society's insurance fund.

If your representative is a consultant practising in Canada

- If your consultant is a member of a professional association in Canada, file a complaint with that association.

- If your consultant is not a member of any association, you might ask the consumer protection office in your province or territory for advice. Some associations might offer to contact the consultant to seek a solution.

- You can report your problem to the Better Business Bureau in the province or territory where your representative works. The BBB might contact your representative to try to resolve the issue for you.

If your representative is either a lawyer or an immigration consultant practising in Canada

- If you believe your representative has committed an offense in the course of representing you, you should go to the local police or to the Royal Canadian Mounted Police.

- If you are in Canada and you wish to recover money you paid for services you did not get, you can file a lawsuit in small claims court. You do not need a lawyer to do so, but you will have to pay a small fee.

- Legal Aid services are available throughout Canada for people who cannot afford to pay for legal assistance. Contact them to see if you qualify for assistance.

If your representative's place of business is abroad

- If your representative is not a Canadian citizen or a permanent resident of Canada, you should present your complaint to the appropriate authorities overseas. The Canadian government cannot get involved in the dispute.

CIC Call Centre

In Montreal: (514) 496-1010

In Toronto: (416) 973-4444

In Vancouver: (604) 666-2171

For all other areas: 1-888-242-2100

PERMANENT RESIDENT CARD

The Permanent Resident Card (also known as the Maple Leaf Card or the PR Card) is a new, wallet-sized, plastic card. People who have completed the Canadian immigration process and have obtained Permanent Resident status, but are not Canadian Citizens can apply for the card. The card replaces the IMM 1000 as the status document needed by Canadian Permanent Residents re-entering Canada on a commercial carrier (airplane, boat, train and bus) as of December 31, 2003.

Security features of the new PR Card will simplify the screening process of Permanent Residents when boarding a commercial carrier going to Canada. The card also increases Canada's border security and improves the integrity of Canada's immigration process.

Beginning on June 28, 2002, PR Cards will be mailed to new Permanent Residents of Canada as part of the landing process. People who are already in Canada as Permanent Residents can apply for the new PR Card beginning October 15, 2002.

About the
Permanent Resident Card

Background

The Canadian government has understood the need for a Permanent Resident Card for quite some time. The events of September 11, 2001 raised the issue of border security and the safety of all Canadians to the forefront. This made the introduction of a PR Card a key government initiative.

Before June 28, 2002, a successful landing application process resulted in the issuing of an IMM 1000 form. This document showed the holder's Canadian entry history. It was a large, difficult-to-carry piece of paper with no photograph, few security features and little in the way of privacy for the Permanent Resident. Technological advancements have made it easy to change, copy or make fraudulent use of many documents, including the IMM 1000.

CIC was intent on finding a replacement for this form that would address convenience, safety, privacy and durability concerns. The new PR Card not only addresses these concerns, but also includes state-of-the-art security features, making it extremely resistant to forgery and alteration.

The new card is a wallet-sized, plastic card, which confirms the Permanent Resident status of the cardholder. It replaces the IMM 1000 Record of Landing Form for travel purposes.

Security Benefits

The new PR Card contains several security features that make it a safe proof of status document for the cardholder. As of December 31, 2003, the new card is a necessary document for every Permanent Resident re-entering Canada by commercial carrier (airplane, boat, train and bus) after international travel.

The card has a laser engraved photograph and signature, as well as a description of the physical characteristics (height, eye colour, gender) of the cardholder printed on the front.

The card's optical stripe will contain all the details from the cardholder's Confirmation of Permanent Resident form. This encrypted information will only be accessible to authorized official (such as immigration officers) as required to confirm the status of the cardholder. The card cannot be used to monitor the activities or track the movement of the cardholder; this will protect the cardholder's privacy.

The card's optical stripe is more advanced than a magnetic stripe (commonly used on bank cards) both in terms of information storage capacity and security of information. Much like a commercial compact disc (CD), it is impossible to change, erase or add to the information already encoded on the optical stripe.

New Immigrants

Beginning on June 28, 2002, all new Permanent Residents will automatically receive their PR Card in the mail following their arrival in Canada. At the point of entry in Canada, personal data will be confirmed as part of the landing process.

If you did not provide your mailing address to CIC at the point of entry, please do so as soon as possible. You can provide this information on-line at http://www.cic.gc.ca/english/e-services/index.html or you can contact the PR Card Call Centre at 1-800-255-4541. Please note that if CIC do not receive your address within 180 days of the date of your admission, you will need to re-apply for your PR Card and pay the applicable fee.

Please notify CIC of any change in your mailing address as soon as possible. You may send them your change of address by mail, or use the on-line Change of Address service.

If you do not receive your PR Card within 30 days after sending CIC your address, please contact CIC Call Centre.

Existing Permanent Residents

PR Cards will be available to Permanent Residents upon application only. CIC will process applications according to a published schedule based on the applicant's year of landing.

There are approximately 1.5 million Permanent Residents in Canada who are eligible to apply for a new PR Card. CIC are committed to processing applications as quickly and efficiently as possible. However, because of the large number of applicants and the short processing period, CIC ask for your patience and understanding should there be delays with your application.

Applications for existing Permanent Residents will be available after September 15, 2002. You can obtain a PR Card Application kit (when available) from CIC website, or by contacting the PR Card Call Centre at 1 800-255-4541 (from Canada & USA) after this date.

CIC will begin processing applications for existing Permanent Residents only after October 15, 2002.

Canadian Citizens

Permanent Resident Cards are not issued to Canadian Citizens. Citizens need a Canadian Passport for international travel.

New PR Card Fees

The PR Card costs $50.00 per applicant. Each person applying for Permanent Residence status in Canada will need a card (children included. The Card is normally valid for five years. All Permanent Residents will need a valid PR Card for re-entry into Canada on a commercial carrier as of December 31, 2003. It will be the cardholder's responsibility to make sure their card will be valid at the time of their return to Canada. If a Permanent Resident with a PR Card has become a Canadian Citizen, the PR Card is automatically cancelled. This person would then need to obtain a Canadian passport for international travel purposes.

Apply for Canadian Citizenship

If you have been a Permanent Resident and have been living in Canada for three years or more, you are eligible to apply for Canadian Citizenship.

What does it mean to be a Canadian citizen?

Citizenship means working together with all other Canadians to build a stronger Canada, and making sure our values, dreams and goals are reflected in our institutions, laws and relations with one another.

After living in Canada for at least three years as a permanent resident, you have the right to apply for Canadian citizenship.

Canada is a country that:

- is free and democratic;
- is multicultural;
- has two official languages; and
- extends equal treatment to all its citizens.

What are the rights and responsibilities of a citizen?

The *Canadian Charter of Rights and Freedoms* sets out the democratic rights and fundamental freedoms of all Canadians. Some rights are essential for Canadian citizens:

- the right to vote or to be a candidate in federal and provincial elections;
- the right to enter, remain in or leave Canada;
- the right to earn a living and reside in any province or territory;
- minority language education rights (English or French); and
- the right to apply for a Canadian passport.

Canadian citizenship also implies the following responsibilities:

- to obey Canada's laws;
- to vote in the federal, provincial and municipal elections;
- to discourage discrimination and injustice;
- to respect the rights of others;
- to respect public and private property; and
- to support Canada's ideals in building the country we all share.

Who is entitled to apply for Canadian citizenship?

You can apply for Canadian citizenship if you:

- are at least 18 years of age;
- have been a legal permanent resident in Canada for three out of the previous four years;
- can communicate in English or French; and
- have knowledge of Canada, including the rights and responsibilities of citizenship.

Who cannot become a Canadian citizen?

You may not be eligible to become a Canadian citizen if you:

- are under a deportation order and are not currently allowed to be in Canada;
- are in prison, on parole or on probation; and
- have been charged or convicted of an indictable offence.

Could you be a Canadian citizen and not know it?

In most cases, you are a Canadian citizen if you were born:

- in Canada, or
- in another country, after February 15, 1977, and have one Canadian parent.

For more information, telephone the Call Centre.

How do you apply for Canadian citizenship?

If you meet the requirements for Canadian citizenship, you can get an "Application for Citizenship" form from the Call Centre, or download an application at http://www.cic.gc.ca.

Fill out the application form and follow the instructions provided. A non-refundable processing fee and a refundable Right of Citizenship fee must be paid at the time of the application. You must include the receipt of payment and necessary documents with your application form.

You will have to take a test to show that you meet the requirements for knowledge of Canada and of either English or French. Study the information in the booklet *A Look at Canada* which will be sent to you with the acknowledgment of your application.

If you meet the basic requirements for citizenship, you will be invited to a citizenship ceremony where you will take the oath and receive your citizenship certificate.

What is dual citizenship?

Dual or plural citizenship means holding citizenship in one or more countries in addition to Canada.

Canada has recognized dual citizenship since 1977. This means that, in some cases, you may become a Canadian citizen while remaining a citizen of another country.

Some countries will not allow their citizens to keep their citizenship if they become citizens of another country. You should check with the embassy or consulate of your country of origin to be sure of their rules and laws.

Where should you go for more information about Canadian citizenship?

If you are in Canada, telephone the Call Centre.

Outside Canada, contact a Canadian embassy or consulate.

How to Apply

Once you have decided that you want to bring your skills to Canada, make sure that you follow the correct steps to apply.

There are a number of steps to follow when you prepare your application as a Skilled Worker. It is important that you carefully read and follow the instructions for each step listed below to ensure that your application is complete and submitted correctly.

Before you start your application, you need the forms that are specific to the Visa Office in your country or region. You will need the forms from your Visa Office for some of the steps below. Look for the checklist in these documents. The checklist will help you make sure that you have completed your application.

Find the checklist and appendixes for the Canadian Visa Office in your country or region.

Step One: Collecting the necessary documents:

It is very important that you include all necessary documentation with your application. Use the Checklist (Appendix A) of the information from your Visa Office to tell you:

- what documents you must include with the application;
- how many copies of each form the visa office needs;
- which documents must be originals and which should be photocopies; and
- if you need to provide a certified translation in English or French

Visa Office Specific Information

Select **only one** of the Visa Office. This is the Visa Office where you will send your application. The documents found here are Appendix A, B and C. You need these documents for your application.

What you need to include with your application can be different depending on where you apply. Read the instructions here carefully. They include:

- a checklist of the documents you need to include with your application;
- information about the medical examination;
- information about obtaining police certificates or clearances; and
- instructions on where to send your application

Select the Visa Office in your geographical region according to your place of residence. Please see the instructions below

Appendix A
Checklist

Assemble all your documents as listed. Check (☑) each applicable item on the checklist and attach it to your documents. Place all the documents in a sealed envelope. Please send **photocopies** of all documents except police certificates, which must be **originals**. If your documents are not in English or French, you must present a notarized (certified) translation with a photocopy of the original.

All documents must be submitted at the same time, together with your completed application form.

1	**FORMS** See the **"Filling Out the Forms"** section on our Web site at www.cic.gc.ca/skilled for specific instructions on how to complete the questions on each of the following forms.	
	APPLICATION FOR PERMANENT RESIDENCE IN CANADA Check that it is complete and signed and that you have included (not stapled) six specified photos (with names on the back for each applicant) for each member of your family and yourself. (See box 14 of this checklist for further information on photo specifications.)	☐
	SCHEDULE 1: BACKGROUND DECLARATION Include a Schedule 1 form completed by: • the principal applicant • spouse or common-law partner • each dependent child over 18 years of age	☐
	SCHEDULE 3: ECONOMIC CLASSES – FEDERAL SKILLED WORKERS Completed by the principal applicant.	☐
	ADDITIONAL FAMILY INFORMATION Completed by: • the principal applicant • spouse or common-law partner • each dependent child over the age of 18 years	☐
	AUTHORITY TO RELEASE INFORMATION TO DESIGNATED INDIVIDUALS Include this form only if you wish us to release information regarding your application to someone other than yourself. Be advised that, if and for as long as you have designated an agent to represent you, we will communicate only with that person or firm. Any processing enquiries you may have must be made through that agent. Any such enquiries that you send directly to this office will neither be answered nor acknowledged.	☐
2	**IDENTITY AND CIVIL STATUS DOCUMENTS** • Birth, marriage, final divorce, annulment or separation certificates for you and your spouse or common-law partner • Death certificate for former spouse if applicable • Photocopy of **citizenship certificate or permanent resident visa** (formerly called "immigrant visa") for any family members who are Canadian citizens or permanent residents of Canada	☐

Note: Checklist and appendices are included in the application forms.

8   **PROOF OF LANGUAGE PROFICIENCY**   ☐

Refer to instructions in the 'Language Assessment Information' section of our Web site at www.cic.gc.ca/skilled. If you are claiming proficiency at any level in English and/or French, submit one of the following:

- **Test results from an approved language-testing organization:** We strongly recommend that you submit test results if you are claiming proficiency in a language that is not your native language. If you choose to send the reports to us directly, you must provide the **original**. Photocopies are unacceptable. Language test results must not be older than one year upon submission.

or

- **Other evidence in writing:**
  - Your written submission detailing your training in, and use of, English and/or French;
  - Official documentation of education in English or French;
  - Official documentation of work experience in English or French.
  - Other applicable documentation.

9   **ARRANGED EMPLOYMENT (if applicable)**   ☐

If you are currently working in Canada under a work permit, provide a photocopy of the permit.

10   **NON-ACCOMPANYING FAMILY MEMBERS DECLARATION (if applicable):**   ☐

If you have a spouse, common-law partner or dependent children and you do not intend to include them in your application for permanent residence, submit with your application a notarized statutory declaration stating your intention to proceed to Canada without your family members, and confirming that you understand that your family members must meet immigration requirements in their own right if they wish to join you in Canada.

11   **SETTLEMENT FUNDS**   ☐

(Refer to the 'Proof of Funds' section of our Web site (www.cic.gc.ca/skilled) or the *Guide for Federal Skilled Worker Applicants* for exact figures and instructions.)

Provide proof of unencumbered and readily transferable funds in a convertible currency available for settlement in Canada (for you and your family members):

- current bank certification letter; or
- evidence of savings balance; or
- fixed or time deposit statements.

12   **POLICE CERTIFICATES AND CLEARANCES**   ☐

- **Original** police certificates of good conduct or clearances, from each country/state/territory in which you and everyone in your family aged 18 years or over have lived for six months or longer since reaching the age of 18.
- Submit original fingerprints directly to the authorities conducting the police checks
- If you have obtained police certificates from countries where the authorities will forward results directly to us, attach a brief explanatory note to your application.

Your local mission may have more detailed instructions about how to obtain police certificates.

13   **FEE PAYMENT**   ☐

Consult the **Fees** section of our Web site or the *Guide for Skilled Worker Applicants* to calculate your fees.

14   **PHOTO REQUIREMENTS**   ☐

Supply the number of photographs requested under **"Application for Permanent Residence in Canada"** in paragraph 1 of the *Checklist* and follow the instructions provided in Appendix C: Photo Specifications.

Appendix B
Obtaining Police Certificates/Clearances

You must provide a police certificate or clearance indicating any criminal record or the absence of a criminal record for yourself, your spouse or common-law partner and all of your dependent children aged 18 and over. You must obtain certificates or clearances from every country in which you or your family members have lived for more than six months since reaching 18 years of age.

It is your responsibility to contact the police or relevant authorities in each of the jurisdictions in which you have lived. You may have to provide information or documentation such as photographs, fingerprints, or your addresses and periods of residence in other countries. You may be asked to pay a fee for the service.

If you have a criminal conviction in Canada, you must seek a pardon from the National Parole Board of Canada before you apply for immigration to Canada. The address is:

Clemency and Pardons Division
National Parole Board
410 Laurier Avenue West
Ottawa, ON, Canada
K1A 0R1
Fax: 1-613-941-4981
Web site: www.npb-cnlc.gc.ca (application forms can be downloaded from the site)

We will also do our own background checks in all countries in which you and your dependants have lived. These checks will determine if you have any arrests or criminal convictions, or if you are a security risk to Canada.

Appendix C
Photo Specifications

Notes to the applicant

TAKE THIS WITH YOU TO THE PHOTOGRAPHER

- Immigration photographs are **not** the same as passport photographs.
- Make sure that you provide the correct number of photographs specified in the *Checklist*.

Notes to the photographer

The photographs must:

- show a full front view of the person's head and shoulders showing full face centred in the middle of the photograph;
- have a **plain white background**;
- be identical (black and white or colour) produced from the same untouched negative, or exposed simultaneously by a split-image or multi-lens camera;

The photographs must:

- measure between 25 mm and 35 mm (1" and 1 3/8") from chin to crown
- have a 35 mm x 45 mm (1 3/8" x 1 3/4") finished size

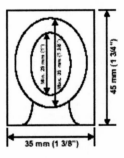

Appendix D
Medical Instructions

You will receive instructions for the medical application in person after the selection interview. If the interview is waived, instructions will be mailed to you after the selection decision has been made.

Step Two: Printing the forms

All of the necessary forms to apply for permanent residence in Canada as a Skilled Worker are available at this site **http://www.cic.gc.ca/english/skilled/forms.html**. You can download and print the forms (quick way) or contact Visa Office in your geographical region according to your place of residence to mail you the application forms. Each form will tell you how many copies you will need.

Step Three: How to Fill Out the Forms

Complete the forms correctly and completely. Incomplete or incorrectly filled out forms will be sent back to you. CIC cannot process incomplete forms.

Step Four: Obtaining Police Certificates:

Get a police certificate or clearance from every country where you or your dependants, aged 18 years or over, lived for six months or longer since reaching the age of 18. You can find instructions in Appendix B of the information.

Step Five: Calculating Fees

- Calculate the fees you must send with your application.
- Prepare the payment. **Do not mail cash.**

Step Six: Verifying the Application

- Use the Checklist (Appendix A) to make sure that you have all of the required documents.
- The Visa Office may request additional information at any time during the application process.

Step Seven: How and where to submit your application

- Use the Checklist (Appendix A) from the information from your Visa Office to make sure your form is complete.
- Submit your completed application to the Visa office dealing in your geographical region.

- Print your name and address on the top left-hand side of the envelope.

The Application Assessment Process

A Visa Office will process your application. The Visa Office may process your application differently depending on your application and the Visa Office. Some processing steps are common to all Visa Offices.

After you submit your application, a Citizenship and Immigration Canada (CIC) officer will check to see that you submitted everything with your application. The officer will make sure that you:

- Completed your application form correctly;
- paid your application fee correctly; and
- included all supporting documentation.

If your application is not complete, CIC will return it to you without starting to process it.

Your Visa Office will send you a letter when they receive your completed application. The letter will tell you what you need to do and what happens next.

Processing Time

The length of time it takes to process your application can be different in each mission or Visa Office. Visit the mission Web site http://www.cic.gc.ca/english/offices/missions.html (if available) where you submitted your application for more information on how long it might take to process your application.

You may be able to speed up the process by:

- making sure all the necessary information is included with your application;
- notifying the Visa Office of any changes to the information on your application;
- avoiding unnecessary enquiries to the Visa Office;

- making sure the photocopies and documents you provide are clear and readable;

- providing certified English or French translations of documents where indicated; and

- applying from a country where you are a citizen or permanent resident.

Your application will be delayed if the Visa Office has to take extra steps to assess your case. Your application will take longer if:

- there are criminal or security problems with your application;

- your family situation is not clear because of a situation such as a divorce or adoption that is not yet complete or child custody issues that have not been resolved; or

- the local Visa Office has to consult with other CIC offices in Canada or abroad.

The Decision on Your Application

The CIC officer will make a decision on your application based on the points you accumulate in the <u>six selection factors</u>. The officer will also evaluate your ability to meet the <u>Required Funds</u> amount for the size of your family.

The Visa Office will contact you if they need more documentation or if you have to come in for a personal interview.

Confirmation of Permanent Residence

You will be given a *Confirmation of Permanent Residence* (COPR) if your application is successful. The COPR will have identification information as well as a photo and your signature. You **must** bring the COPR to the Port of Entry with your visa when you enter Canada.

Checking the Status of Your Application

Once you have received notice from our office that your application has been received, you can check the status of your application online at http://www.cic.gc.ca/english/e-services/index.html

A Word For A Wise

You may feel that it is very difficult to prepare immigration application by yourself but when you will go through the whole contents of the checklists, you will understand the exact requirements to prepare and submit your application. Start preparing your required documents one by one. You will observe that its very easy and simple. Just go through each and every item on checklist at least twice. Most of skilled workers prepare their immigration cases by themselves and save considerable amount of professional fee ranging from US$ 2000-4000

What if I don't want to take IELTS Test

If you think that you are proficient enough in English language and have a certificate or diploma in English language training from a reputable institute of you country or your mother tongue is English by birth and you do not want to take IELTS test then you can try and submit following explanation. This is a specimen, you can re-write it according to your situation. Further, it's the discretion of visa officer to accept or reject your explanation to award the necessary points for your English language ability or can instruct you to take official IELTS test and submit the results.

A SPECIMEN OF EXPLANATION OF ENGLISH LANGUAGE PROFICIENCY AND EXPERIENCE

My Training in English Language

My training in English language starts from my 1st grade at school and gradually refined and master it by the passage of time up to my university level. English Language was the medium of instruction throughout my academics. I have to Read, Write, Speak and Listen in English language everyday.

How Commonly I use English

Being a professional and spending most of my time at work, English is the dominating language that I have to use throughout the day. Following is my caliber with regard to proficiency in English language.

Speaking

- I can communicate effectively in most daily practical and social situations, and in familiar routine work situations with my colleagues and my superiors

- I can participate in conversations with confidence

- I can speak on familiar topics at both concrete and abstract levels (20 to 30 minutes). As I often need to do presentations for foreign delegates about the deployment of I.T and new technologies in our organization.

- I can provide descriptions, opinions and explanations; can synthesize abstract complex ideas and can hypothesize.

- In social interaction, I demonstrate increased ability to respond appropriately to the formality level of the situation.

- I can use a variety of sentence structures, including embedded and report structures, and an expanded inventory of concrete, idiomatic and conceptual language in my routine progress meetings with staff and directors.

- My discourse is reasonably fluent. Grammar and pronunciation errors rarely impede my communication. I also use phone on less familiar and some non-routine matters.

Listening

- I can comprehend main points, details, speaker's purpose, attitudes, levels of formality and styles in oral discourse in moderately demanding contexts.

- I can follow most formal and informal conversations, and some technical work-related discourse in my field at a normal rate of speech.

- I can follow discourse about abstract and complex ideas on a familiar topic.

- I can comprehend an expanded range of concrete, abstract and conceptual language.

- I can determine mood, attitudes and feelings.

- I can understand sufficient vocabulary, idioms and colloquial expressions to follow detailed stories of general popular interest.

- I can follow clear and coherent extended instructional texts and directions.

- I can follow clear and coherent phone messages on unfamiliar and non-routine matters.

Reading

- I can follow main ideas, key words and important details in an authentic four to six page text on a familiar topic.

- I can read popular newspaper and international magazines (Time, Newsweek, Reader Digest). I can read general / technical articles and popular easy fiction as well as academic and business materials.

- I can extract relevant points, but sometime require clarification of idioms and of various cultural references.

- I can locate and integrate several specific pieces of information in visually complex texts (e.g., tables, directories) or across paragraphs or sections of text. That text can be on abstract, conceptual or technical topics, containing facts, attitudes and opinions.

- I also use a unilingual dictionary when reading for precision vocabulary building

Writing

- I have demonstrated fluent ability in performing moderately comple: writing tasks like in my technology reports.

- I can link sentences and paragraphs (three or four) to form coheren texts to express ideas on familiar abstract topics, with some suppo for main ideas, and with an appropriate sense of audience.

- I can write routine business letters (e.g., letters of inquiry, cove letters for applications) and personal and formal social messages.

- I can write down a set of simple instructions, based on clear or communication or simple written procedural text of greater length.

- I can fill out complex formatted documents.

- I can extract key information and relevant detail from a page-lon text and write an outline or a one-paragraph summary.

- I have demonstrated good control over common sentence patterns coordination and subordination, and spelling and mechanics. in m professional report writing.

Official Documentation Of Education In English Language

Please find attached attested copy of my diploma in English language from a well-known institution in which I have **scored 90% marks with "A+" grade**.

Your Signature

Peter Burt

A NEWCOMER'S INTRODUCTION TO CANADA

FOREWORD

Congratulations! You are taking a big step. Moving to a new country offers exciting opportunities and new beginnings!

This information will help you get ready to leave your home country and make a new life in Canada. It tells you what documents you will need to bring, what to expect in the first few days and weeks, how to find a place to live, get a Social Insurance Number and a health-care card, and find a job. It also explains what services you can expect to receive from the immigrant-serving organizations across Canada. You will also find useful information about Canada's geography, history, government and way of life, and about how to become a Canadian citizen.

A Newcomer's Introduction to Canada was written to give you helpful information for planning ahead, but it is not a detailed guide. When you arrive in Canada, you will be given a book called *Welcome to Canada: What You Should Know*. **http://www.cic.gc.ca/english/newcomer/welcome/index.html**. It contains specific information on all the practical aspects of living in Canada.

A Newcomer's Introduction to Canada will not answer all of your questions, but it is a good place to start.

TABLE OF CONTENTS

FINDING A JOB, BUILDING A FUTURE

- International educational assessment services in Canada
- Provincial evaluation services
- Employment in regulated professions and trades
- Language skills
- Job opportunities
- Employment laws
- Discrimination
- Deductions and taxable benefits
  - Income tax
  - Canada Pension Plan
  - Employment Insurance
  - Taxable benefits
  - Union dues

GENERAL INFORMATION ABOUT CANADA

- Geography
- Distances
- Population
- Map of Canada
- The Francophone population
- History
- Economy
- Government
- Federal government
- Provincial governments
- Territorial governments
- Municipal governments
- Bilingualism
- Multiculturalism
- Protecting the environment -- Sustainable development

THE CANADIAN WAY OF LIFE

- o Family life and family law
- o Marriage, divorce and the law
- o Birth control and family planning
- o Youth and their parents
- o Youth and the law
- Standards and expectations
  - o Important social standards
- Some Canadian laws
- Interacting with officials
  - o People in authority
  - o Public officials
  - o Police officers

YOUR RIGHTS AND OBLIGATIONS

- Personal rights and freedoms
- Children's rights
- Women's rights
- Senior citizens' rights
- Becoming a Canadian citizen
- Responsible and active citizenship

AFTERWORD

GETTING READY -- BEFORE YOU LEAVE FOR CANADA

- **Essential documents**
- **Important documents**
- **What you should know about health care**
- **What you can bring into Canada**
- **Getting ready to look for work**
- **Getting ready if you are a business immigrant**
- **Communities across Canada**
- **The Canadian climate: What to expect and what clothes to bring**
- **Schools and universities**

Essential Documents

When you travel to Canada, you will need to have the following documents with you:

- a Canadian immigrant visa and Confirmation of Permanent Residence for each family member travelling with you;
- a valid passport or other travel document for each family member travelling with you;
- two copies of a detailed list of all the personal or household items you are bringing with you; and
- two copies of a list of items that are arriving later.

Note: The lists should state how much your personal and household items are worth.

- You must also bring with you enough money to cover living expenses such as rent, food, clothing and transportation for a six-month period. You may be asked to show proof of your funds.

Do not pack your documents in a suitcase. You will need to have them available to show to immigration and customs officials.

> **TIP !** Make two copies of these lists -- one for you to keep and one for the Canada Customs officer. You can get the Canada Customs and Revenue Agency form for this purpose from the Internet at www.ccra-adrc.gc.ca/E/pbg/cf/b4abq

Important documents

Depending on your personal situation, you should bring the following important documents with you to Canada:

- birth certificates or baptismal certificates;
- marriage certificates;
- adoption, separation or divorce papers;
- school records, diplomas or degrees for each family member travelling with you;
- trade or professional certificates and licences;
- letters of reference from former employers;
- a list of your educational and professional qualifications and job experience (this is also called a résumé);
- immunization, vaccination, dental and other health records for each family member;
- driver's licence, including an International Driver's Permit, and a reference from your insurance company;
- photocopies of all essential and important documents, in case the originals get lost (be sure to keep the photocopies in a separate place from the originals); and

113

- car registration documents (if you are importing a motor vehicle into Canada).

> **TIP** ! If possible, get all of your documents translated into English or French by a qualified translator before you leave for Canada.

What You Should Know About Health Care

Canada has a public health-care system known as "medicare." It provides insurance coverage for health-care services to all Canadian citizens and permanent residents. (You will be a "permanent resident.") The federal government sets health-care standards for the whole country, but the programs are run by the provincial ministries of health. More information on the health-care system can be found in *Your first few days in Canada*.

> **TIP** ! Apply for provincial health-care coverage as soon as possible after you arrive in the province where you plan to live.

Note: British Columbia, Ontario, Quebec and New Brunswick have a three month waiting period before you become eligible for medicare coverage. If you are planning to settle in any of these provinces, you should buy private health insurance coverage for the first three months. Insurance companies are listed in the Yellow Pages of all Canadian telephone books, under "Insurance."

> **TIP** ! Bring a supply of your medications with you to allow you time to find a family doctor in Canada from whom you will have to get new prescriptions.

What You Can Bring Into Canada

There are strict laws about what you can bring into Canada.

Cars must meet Canadian safety and pollution control standards. Many cars are not allowed into the country. Contact Transport Canada for more information before you ship your car.

> Transport Canada, Vehicle Importation
> 330 Sparks Street, Tower C
> Ottawa, Ontario K1A 0N5
>
> Telephone: 1 (613) 998-8616
> (when calling from outside Canada)
>
> 1 800 333-0371
> (toll-free, from inside Canada)
>
> Web site: **www.tc.gc.ca**
>
> (follow the link to Vehicle Importation)

The following items cannot be brought into Canada:

- unauthorized firearms, explosives, fireworks and ammunition;
- narcotics, other than prescription drugs;
- meat, dairy products, fresh fruits and vegetables;
- plants, flowers and soil;
- endangered species of animals or products made from animal parts, such as the skin, feathers, fur, bones and ivory;
- cultural property, including antique and cultural objects considered to have historical significance in their country of origin (you may, however, bring family heirlooms);
- more than 200 cigarettes (you must pay tax on the excess amount) per person over 18 years of age if you are immigrating to Quebec, Alberta, Saskatchewan or Manitoba, or per person over

19 if you are immigrating to Ontario or any of the other provinces and

- more than 1.5 litres of commercial alcohol (you must pay tax on the excess amount) per person over 19 years of age.

If you are not sure about an item, you can write to or telephone:

Canada Customs and Revenue Agency
Customs, Excise and Taxation
Information Services
2265 St. Laurent Boulevard
Ottawa, Ontario K1G 4K3

Telephone: 1 (506) 636-5064
(when calling from outside Canada)

1 800 461-9999
(toll-free, from inside Canada)

Web site: **www.ccra-adrc.gc.ca**

Getting Ready To Look For Work

If possible, have your documents translated into English or French before you leave for Canada. Essential documents for looking for work include:

- a résumé of your education, work and volunteer experience, and your skills and qualifications;
- diplomas, degrees, certificates and other qualifications;
- letters of recommendation; and
- school records or transcripts.

> **TIP !** Improving your English or French before coming to Canada would be extremely beneficial.

Research the labour market in the part of Canada where you plan to settle. The following federally funded Web sites will be helpful:

- **www.workinfonet.ca:** This is a national Web site for career and labour market information. It contains job information for each province and territory. It also contains information on self-employment, education and training.

- **www.workdestinations.org:** This Web site contains information on various jobs, working conditions, labour market trends, living conditions, and training and educational opportunities in different regions of Canada. It also lists regulated jobs in Canada. You can find out whether your job is regulated and what you will need to do to get a licence to practise.

- **lmi-imt.hrdc-drhc.gc.ca:** This Web site offers labour market information, which can help you search for work and make general employment, training and career decisions.

- **workplace.hrdc-drhc.gc.ca/page2.asp?sect=1:** This Web site offers links to Canadian newspapers' on-line "Help Wanted" advertisements.

- **www.worksitecanada.com/news:** This Web site links to the employment section in the classified advertisements pages of Canada's daily newspapers to give you an idea of the jobs available now.

TIP ! To be better prepared to look for work in Canada, have your credentials evaluated and compared with the Canadian education system to make it easier for employers to determine whether you meet their job requirements. See *International educational assessment services in Canada.*

TIP ! Professionals in government-regulated occupations should contact the licensing body in their province of destination. See *Employment in regulated professions and trades.*

Getting Ready If You Are
A Business Immigrant

If you are coming to Canada as a business immigrant, use the Internet to find out about sources of financing, business opportunities, export and investment services, self-employment assistance and information for small businesses. There are many rules for starting a business in Canada. The following Government of Canada Web sites will help you get a head start in your planning:

- **www.cbsc.org:** The Canada Business Service Centre's Web site is your single point of contact for information on government services programs and rules for business.

- **www.strategis.gc.ca:** This Industry Canada Web site has business information to help you find partners, do market research, find new technologies, and learn about financing opportunities and growth areas in the Canadian economy.

- **www.bdc.ca:** This is the Web site of the Business Development Bank of Canada. It provides financial and consulting services to Canadian small businesses, especially those in the technology and export sectors of the economy. It also offers information on how to start a business and make it succeed.

- **http://strategis.ic.gc.ca/sc_mangb/smallbus/engdoc/sbla.html:** This is the Web site of the Canada Small Business Financing Program. The program can help you finance your own business.

- **www.contractscanada.gc.ca:** This Web site has information on how and what the Government of Canada buys (both goods and services).

- **www.cic.gc.ca:** This is the Web site of Citizenship and Immigration Canada. It describes the Business Immigration Program. You will find many answers to your questions at this site.

> **TIP !** When you are deciding how much money to bring into Canada, it helps to research the cost of living in the part of Canada where you plan to live. This information can be found on the provincial and territorial Web sites at canada.gc.ca/othergov/prov_e.html.

Communities Across Canada

Most newcomers to Canada tend to settle in the three biggest cities -- Toronto, Montréal and Vancouver. But many newcomers and many Canadians choose to live in the medium-sized cities, which they feel have as much to offer as the larger cities with a better quality of life.

Among the medium-sized cities are Halifax, Québec City, Ottawa, London, Windsor, Sudbury, Winnipeg, Saskatoon, Regina, Calgary and Edmonton.

All of the medium-sized cities have diverse, multi-ethnic populations ranging in size from approximately 100,000 to one million people, and all have the variety of public and private institutions and services found in the largest cities.

> **TIP !** To locate the medium-sized cities on a map of Canada, go to *Map of Canada*.

Some newcomers like the idea of living in smaller cities or towns like Moncton, Fredericton and Victoria, or prefer to live in a rural area. Depending on your skills or professional qualifications, some regions may have better job opportunities than others.

> **TIP !** Outside the larger cities, the costs of housing, higher education and services are often much lower.

If you use the Internet, visit the Web sites of each province and territory to see what each has to offer. To find these Web sites, visit **canada.gc.ca/othergov/prov_e.html**.

Each Web site has a list of government departments and agencies. In the bigger provinces, some government departments may have their own Web sites, with more detailed information. You may also find a directory of on-line services, a link to educational institutions, and a link to major cities and towns. Most of the Web sites also have a tourism section, where you can discover the special attractions of each province and territory.

As mentioned earlier in this chapter, the Web site www.workdestinations.org has links to information on the labour market and the housing market of communities across Canada. It also has useful tips and information about moving within Canada.

You can also visit a Web site called Canadian Government Information on the Internet at **www.cgii.gc.ca.** It is another useful link to federal, provincial and municipal government information.

> **TIP !** Research carefully the labour market trends or access to your profession in the province and city where you wish to live.

> **TIP !** Most Web sites have a search engine. When you click on the search button, you can look for specific information on immigration, multiculturalism, citizenship, education, training, employment, housing, labour, health, employment opportunities or jobs by typing in these key words.

The Canadian Climate: What To Expect And What Clothes To Bring

Most of Canada has four distinct seasons: spring, summer, autumn and winter. The temperatures and weather in each season can be different from one part of the country to another. Here is what you can expect:

Spring: Spring is a rainy season in most parts of Canada. Daytime temperatures rise steadily, but the nights remain cool. Average daytime temperatures are about 12°C in March, April and early May.

Summer: Summer officially begins on June 21, but July and August are summer for most Canadians. In summer, the weather is very warm in most parts of the country. In southern Canada, daytime temperatures are normally above 20°C and can sometimes rise above 30°C.

Autumn: The autumn season, or fall, as it's often called, begins in September. The weather cools and the leaves on many trees change colour and fall to the ground. It can also be very rainy at this time of year. In some parts of Canada, especially northern or mountain regions, snow may begin to fall by late October. Average daytime temperatures are about 10°C to 12°C in most of the country. The autumn months are September, October and November.

Winter: During the winter months (December, January and February), the temperature in most of the country usually stays below 0°C, day and night. Temperatures in some parts of the country periodically drop below -25°C, while along the West Coast, the temperature rarely drops below 0°C. In most of Canada, snow will be on the ground from mid-December to the middle of March. The higher in elevation and the farther north you go, the longer and colder winter becomes.

TIP ! If you arrive in Canada in the winter, you will need warm clothing such as insulated, waterproof boots; an overcoat; a scarf for your neck; a hat that covers your ears; and gloves or mittens. If you come from a warm climate, buy some winter clothes before you leave for Canada, if possible. Or, be ready to buy winter clothes soon after arriving (note also that winter clothes are more expensive than summer clothes). You may wish to contact an immigrant-serving organization in your new community for help.

TIP ! You can find detailed weather information for each region of Canada on the Environment Canada Web site: weatheroffice.ec.gc.ca.

Schools And Universities

There is no national school system in Canada. Schools and universities are run by the provinces; therefore, education varies somewhat from province to province. Most elementary and secondary schooling is public, meaning it is free and open to everyone.

Depending on the individual province, primary education starts at pre kindergarten and continues to the end of grade 6 or 8. This is followed by secondary education or high school. In some provinces this may be divided into junior high (grades 7 to 9) and senior high (grades 10 to 12). Normally students must complete the required academic courses in high school in order to be admitted to university or college.

The regular school year runs from late August or early September until mid to late June. New students can usually be registered throughout the school year. Most schools are closed on national holidays. Also, all schools are closed between Christmas Eve and New Year's Day, and most are closed for a week in March for spring break. The longest school holiday occurs over the summer months of July and August.

Universities and community colleges hold their regular classes from late August or early September until April, although some courses are offered from January to April and a smaller number are available over the summer months. University and community college courses are not free and the costs vary among the provinces.

When you register your children at the local school or school board office you must take with you:

- Canadian immigrant visa (Record of Landing);
- birth certificate or baptismal certificate;
- vaccination certificate;
- any previous school records.

Your children's language and mathematical skills will be assessed, if necessary, and they will be placed in the program the school thinks is best for them.

> **TIP !** For information about the educational system in Canada, visit the provincial or territorial Web sites at canada.gc.ca/othergov/prov_e.html, or visit ceris.schoolnet.ca/e/, www.aucc.ca or www.accc.ca.

> **TIP !** Education in Canada is available in English and French. Many Canadian parents, even if they do not speak French themselves, believe it is good for their children to be able to speak both English and French. Some put their children in a French immersion program, where children learn most of the regular subjects in French.

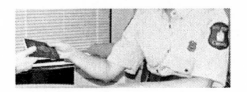

THE DAY YOU ARRIVE IN CANADA

- **Customs and immigration**
- **Reception services**

Customs and immigration

You will probably find the entry procedure fairly straightforward because you have a passport and other <u>essential documents</u>.

You will be interviewed by a Canada Customs officer. You will need to give the officer a list of all the household and personal items that you will be bringing into Canada. You should also show the immigrant visa to the customs officer, who will refer you to an immigration officer.

The immigration officer will check your visa and travel documents and ask you questions similar to those on the Immigrant Application Form, to verify that you are of good character and in good health. At this time, you may also be asked to show proof of your funds. If there are no difficulties, the officer will authorize your entry to Canada as a permanent resident by signing your Record of Landing or Confirmation of Permanent Residence.

If you arrive at one of the major Canadian airports, you will get a booklet called *Welcome to Canada: What You Should Know*. It has information on most aspects of life in Canada. It also provides addresses and telephone numbers for:

- immigrant-serving organizations across Canada;
- language training assessment centres (which help eligible adult newcomers find free language classes);
- useful federal and provincial government offices.

124

Reception Services

If you arrive in Toronto, Montréal or Vancouver, you will find immigrant reception services in the airport. These services are run by immigrant-serving organizations. They help newcomers get the information and services they need, and this help is often available in several languages. In Montréal, the *Ministère des Relations avec les citoyens et de l'Immigration* runs this service.

> **TIP !** *Welcome to Canada: What You Should Know* and other useful information for newcomers can be found on the Internet at www.cic.gc.ca/english/newcomer, and at www.directioncanada.gc.ca

IMMIGRANT-SERVING ORGANIZATIONS

- **LINC (Language Instruction for Newcomers to Canada)**
- **Host Program**

There are hundreds of immigrant-serving organizations in Canada. Many are staffed by former newcomers to Canada, who understand the challenges that immigrants may face. They usually have people available who speak your language and can accompany you as interpreters. Citizenship and Immigration Canada supports many of these organizations financially, helping newcomers adapt to life in Canada.

Settling in will be much easier if you contact an immigrant-serving organization as soon as you arrive. The people who work for these organizations can help you find a place to live and can answer your questions about shopping, education for your children, transportation, language training and other important matters.

Immigrant-serving organizations can help you:

- find a place to live;
- get your Social Insurance Number and health-care card;
- enroll your children in school;
- get language training;
- find a family doctor;
- find out about government and community services for newcomers;
- look for a job;
- develop a realistic budget; and
- get emergency food aid, if it is needed.

Note: In Quebec, the *Ministère des Relations avec les citoyens et de l'Immigration* is organized into different regions. Each region has a local office, called a *Carrefour d'intégration,* which works with the immigrant-serving organizations to help newcomers adapt to life in Quebec.

Most immigrant-serving organizations offer, or can provide information on, the following Government of Canada programs:

LINC (Language Instruction for Newcomers to Canada)

LINC is a federal government program for all eligible adult immigrants. It offers:

- free language training for adult newcomers who want or need basic English or French;

- language classes given by school boards, colleges and local organizations;

- the choice of studying part time, full time, evenings or weekends, depending on your needs and your schedule; and

- transportation and child-minding, if necessary.

> **TIP !** Your local immigrant-serving organization can direct you to a LINC Assessment Centre, which will then refer you to organizations offering LINC classes. You can also refer to the book *Welcome to Canada: What You Should Know* to find a LINC Assessment Centre in your area.

Host Program

The Host Program is a federally funded program that matches newcomers with a Canadian family or individual. Host volunteers help you:

- overcome the stress of moving to a new country;

- learn about available services and how to use them;

- practise English or French;
- prepare to look for a job; and
- participate in community activities.

> **TIP !** Your local immigrant-serving organization can direct you to a Host Program organization in your community.

Immigrant-serving organizations are prepared to help newcomers as soor as they arrive in Canada. These organizations can:

- refer you to economic, social, health, cultural, educational anc recreational services;
- give you tips on banking, shopping, managing a household anc other everyday tasks;
- provide interpreters or translators, if you need them;
- provide non-therapeutic counselling; and
- help you prepare a professional-looking résumé and learn job searching skills.

The Immigrant Settlement and Adaptation Program (ISAP), a federal government program, pays for these services.

A list of immigrant-serving organizations across Canada can be found or the Internet at **www.cic.gc.ca/english/newcomer/welcome/wel-20e.html**

> **TIP !** Manitoba, British Columbia and Quebec have programs similar to LINC, the Host Program and ISAP, but they may have slightly different names.

YOUR FIRST FEW DAYS IN CANADA

- **Finding a place to live**
  - ○ **To buy or to rent**
  - ○ **Types of housing**
  - ○ **How to find a place to live**
  - ○ **What if you have a large family?**
  - ○ **How much will it cost?**
  - ○ **Signing a lease**
- **Applying for a health-insurance card**
- **Applying for a Social Insurance Number**

FINDING A PLACE TO LIVE

To buy or to rent

When you first arrive in Canada, you will probably be living in a temporary home. You will soon be looking for a more permanent place to live. Canada has many different types of housing and a wide range of prices. Finding the right place will take some time and effort. Your first decision will be whether to rent a house or an apartment, or to buy a house.

Whether you rent or buy will depend on your personal finances and whether you already have a job in Canada. Most newcomers decide they should first rent a house or apartment. This gives them more time to save money to buy a house and to decide where they want to live.

If you want to buy a house, unless you can pay the full price, you will need to get a long-term loan called a mortgage. Mortgage loans are provided by banks and other financial institutions. They decide whether the borrower has enough income, more assets than debts, and a good credit rating. Most will ask you to pay at least 10 percent of the cost of the house from your own money.

Types of housing

- **Furnished or unfurnished:** Furnished housing should include beds, tables, chairs, lamps, curtains, a stove and a refrigerator. Unfurnished housing may include a stove and a refrigerator, but not always.

- **Room for rent:** This is usually in a house or an apartment that is owned or rented by other people. Everyone shares the kitchen and bathrooms.

- **Bachelor or studio apartment:** These are small apartments designed mainly for one person. They have one large room with a kitchen and a sleeping area, plus a separate bathroom.

- **Other apartments:** Most other apartments have from one to three bedrooms. All will have a separate kitchen, a living room and a bathroom.

- **Duplex:** This is a house divided into two separate apartments. It may be bought or rented.

- **Townhouse:** This is a small house joined to other houses. It may be bought or rented.

- **Condominium:** This is an apartment or townhouse that is individually owned, while "common areas" are jointly owned. As well as the mortgage payment and property taxes, each owner pays a monthly fee for maintenance, such as snow removal, grass cutting and repairs.

How To Find A Place To Live

Here's how to look for the right home for you:

- search the classified advertisements in local newspapers;
- become familiar with the public transportation available;
- ask an immigrant-serving organization in your area for advice;
- ask friends and family already living in the area for advice;
- look for "Vacancy" or "For Rent" signs on houses and apartment buildings;
- check bulletin boards in grocery stores, Laundromats, health clinics and community centres; and
- ask for advice at your place of worship.

What if you have a large family?

If you have three or more children, or you have older relatives living with you, you will probably not be able to find a big enough apartment. In that case, you may need to think about renting a house.

How much will it cost?

You could expect to pay between $350 a month for a room, and $2,000 a month for a luxury apartment or a large house. Rental costs vary greatly across cities and across Canada. Housing is more reasonable outside the large cities. An immigrant-serving organization in the area where you plan to settle can help you find affordable housing.

Signing a lease

Once you agree to rent an apartment or a house, you may be asked to sign a one-year lease. This legal document of one or two pages describes the rental property, the utilities included and the options, such as parking and storage. It may also state whether pets or more people are allowed. Most apartments are leased by the year, although some are rented monthly.

You will probably need to pay the first and last month's rent when you sign the lease.

If your apartment requires a lease, your landlord will give you the lease form to sign. Read it over carefully before you sign it. Pay special attention to the parts that state exceptions and additions. You should know which utilities you will pay for and which ones will be paid for by the landlord. Be sure you know what the monthly rent payment includes. For example, is the electricity included? the water included? the parking included?

Also find out whether you have to pay a fee if you leave before the lease term is over. You cannot usually break a lease agreement. It is also likely you will be asked to provide a Canadian reference or to have a co-signer sign the lease to guarantee your financial commitment.

If you don't understand some of the legal terms used in the lease document contact one of the groups that help immigrants, or someone you know and trust who can help you. Once you sign the lease, it is a legal document.

TIP ! As people in Canada tend to move in the spring and summer months, these are the best times to look for a home; there will be more choices available.

TIP ! Plan on spending 35 to 50 percent of your income on housing. This should include the cost of electricity, heating, telephone service and water. To find out more before you arrive in Canada, visit the Web site www.cic.gc.ca or www.cmhc-schl.gc.ca/en/bureho/reho

---

APPLYING FOR A HEALTH INSURANCE CARD

One of the most important things you need to do as soon as you arrive in Canada is to apply for a health insurance card. All members of your family, even newborn babies, must have their own card. You can get an application form from the provincial ministry of health office, any doctor's office, a hospital or a pharmacy. If necessary, the immigrant-serving organization in your area can help you fill out the form. To apply for a health card, you will need your birth certificate, Record of Landing (IMM 1000) or Confirmation of Permanent Residence (IMM 5292) and passport. The Permanent Residence card may also be presented. In most provinces, you will receive coverage as soon as you apply.

> **TIP !** In Ontario, British Columbia, New Brunswick and Quebec, there is a three-month waiting period before you become eligible for medicare coverage. If you are immigrating to any of these provinces, you should get private, short-term health-care insurance for the first three months. Insurance companies are listed in the Yellow Pages of all Canadian telephone books, under "Insurance."

Health-care services covered by medicare include:

- examination and treatment by family doctors;
- many types of surgery;
- most treatment by specialists;
- hospital care;
- X-rays;
- many laboratory tests; and
- most immunizations.

Health-care services not covered by medicare, and for which you will have to pay, include:

- ambulance services;
- prescription drugs;
- dental care; and
- glasses and contact lenses.

These services are sometimes covered by workplace benefit packages.

Your health insurance card is mainly for use in the province where you live If you are visiting another province and have a medical emergency, you car use your card. However, if you move to another province, you will need to apply for a new card.

APPLYING FOR A SOCIAL INSURANCE NUMBER

To work in Canada, you must have a Social Insurance Number. This is a nine-digit number that you will need to look for a job and to receive government benefits. Sometimes, you will hear people call it the SIN number. You can get a SIN application form through the Human Resources Development Canada Centre near you. These centres are run by the federal government. You can also get a form through your local immigrant-serving organization or from the post office, or you can download one from the Internet at **www.hrdc-drhc.gc.ca/sin-nas**. The SIN card will be sent to you in the mail. There is a small fee for processing the application.

> **TIP !** To find the nearest Human Resources Centre, look in the Blue Pages of any telephone book under "Government of Canada -- Employment," or go on the Internet at www.hrdc-drhc.gc.ca/menu/profile-search.shtml#100

FINDING A JOB, BUILDING A FUTURE

- **International educational assessment services in Canada**
- **Provincial evaluation services**
- **Employment in regulated professions and trades**
- **Language skills**
- **Job opportunities**
- **Employment laws**
- **Discrimination**
- **Deductions and taxable benefits**
  - **Income tax**
  - **Canada Pension Plan**
  - **Employment Insurance**
  - **Taxable benefits**
  - **Union dues**

In Canada, full-time jobs are common. However, a growing number of people have part-time or short-term jobs. Women make up a large portion of the work force and many have important, senior positions.

Canadians may change jobs and careers several times. This is often a personal choice. Sometimes people must change jobs because the economy changes. For these, and other reasons, getting a job is not easy. Many people are looking for work.

Newcomers to Canada rarely enter the job market quickly and often must start with jobs below the skill level they worked at in their home country.

Once they have Canadian job experience and their ability in English or French improves, so do their job prospects.

International educational assessment services in Canada

Even if you have many years of experience, you do not automatically have the right to practise your trade or profession in Canada. In most cases, you will need to have your credentials assessed to see whether you need more training, education or Canadian work experience before being qualified to practise. You may wish to get your credentials evaluated before you leave for Canada. The following organizations can tell you how to get your credentials assessed:

The Canadian Information Centre for International Credentials Web site (www.cicic.ca) has information on academic and occupational credentials for all of Canada and lists nearly 100 professions and trades, in alphabetical order. When you click on your profession or trade, you will find a link to the address and telephone number of the professional or trade association, the addresses and telephone numbers of provincial evaluation services and regulatory agencies, and labour market information (for example, whether there is a demand for people with your particular trade or profession). You will also be able to find out whether your profession or trade is regulated.

The Centre does not grant equivalencies or assess credentials. It gives advice and refers newcomers to sources of help. To contact the Centre by mail, write to:

Canadian Information Centre for International Credentials

95 St. Clair Avenue West, Suite 1106
Toronto, Ontario M4V 1N6
Telephone: 1 (416) 962-9725
Fax: 1 (416) 962-2800
E-mail: info@cicic.ca
URL: **www.cicic.ca**

Provincial evaluation services

World Education Services assesses academic credentials for a fee. Its assessment will tell you how your education compares with educational standards in the province where you are planning to settle. You can give your assessment to any employer in Canada. It may help you in your job search. To contact World Education Services, write to:

**World Education Services Academic
Credential Assessment Service**
45 Charles Street East, Suite 700
Toronto, Ontario
M4Y 1S2 Canada
Telephone: 1 (416) 972-0070
Toll-free: 1 866 343-0070 (within Canada)
Fax: 1 (416) 972-9004
E-mail: ontario@wes.org
URL: **www.wes.org/ca**

**Education Credentials Evaluation
(Service des équivalences d'études)**
Ministère des Relations avec les citoyens
et de l'Immigration
Suite 200
800, De Maisonneuve Boulevard East
Montréal, Quebec
H2L 4L8 Canada
Telephone: 1 (514) 864-9191
Toll-free: 1 877 264-6164 (within Canada)
Fax: 1 (514) 873-8701
E-mail: equivalences@mrci.gouv.qc.ca
URL: **www.immq.gouv.qc.ca/equivalences**

**International Qualifications
Assessment Service**
Ministry of Learning
Government of Alberta
4th Floor, Sterling Place
9940-106 Street
Edmonton, Alberta
T5K 2N2 Canada
Telephone: 1 (780) 427-2655
Fax: 1 (780) 422-9734
E-mail: iqas@gov.ab.ca
URL: **www.learning.gov.ab.ca/iqas/iqas.asp**

International Credential Evaluation Service
4355 Mathissi Place
Burnaby, British Columbia
V5G 4S8 Canada

Telephone: 1 (604) 431-3402

Fax: 1 (604) 431-3382

E-mail: icesinfo@ola.bc.ca
URL: **www.ola.bc.ca/ices**

Manitoba Credentials
Recognition Program
Manitoba Culture, Heritage and Citizenship
Settlement and Labour Market
Services Branch
5th Floor, 213 Notre Dame Avenue
Winnipeg, Manitoba
R3B 1N3 Canada
Telephone: 1 (204) 945-6300 or
1 (204) 945-3162
Fax: 1 (204) 948-2256
E-mail: immigratemanitoba@gov.mb.ca
URL: ***www.gov.mb.ca/labour/immigrate/newcomerservices/7c.html***

Employment In Regulated
Professions And Trades

In Canada, about 20 percent of jobs are regulated by the government to protect public health and safety. For example, nurses, doctors, engineers, teachers and electricians all work in regulated professions. People who want to work in regulated jobs need to get a licence from the regulatory body in the province in which they live. If you want to know more about how to enter a particular profession or trade in a particular province, you should contact the provincial regulatory body for that job. The professions are self regulating and they administer the provincial laws that apply to their profession. Rules for entering professions also differ from province to province. (For more information, visit **www.cicic.ca**.)

> **TIP !** Regulated occupations in Canada usually require many years of education, training and practical experience, and the successful completion of a technical examination. Technical examinations to enter a trade or profession can be very expensive.

138

Language Skills

It is important to learn English or French as quickly as possible. Many newcomers begin life in Canada by looking for a job that will allow them to learn or improve their English or French. The <u>Language Instruction for Newcomers to Canada (LINC)</u> program gives eligible adult immigrants the chance to take basic English or French classes at no charge.

People with foreign credentials need a Test of English as a Foreign Language (TOEFL) score to enter Canadian colleges and universities. Colleges and universities offering courses in French use various French language tests.

> **TIP !** Look into taking English classes through the LINC Program.

Job Opportunities

- **Human Resources Development Canada Centres:** Counsellors at these centres can give you free advice and information about job and language training and work creation programs for newcomers. They can help you plan an effective job search and prepare a résumé of your education and experience. Each centre also has listings of available jobs on computer or on bulletin boards.

- **Classified advertisements:** Every daily newspaper in Canada has a classified advertisements section where you will find a variety of jobs listed. In many areas, there are also weekly or monthly employment papers that advertise jobs.

- **Local help:** To help newcomers prepare to enter the Canadian work force or to gain access to their profession or trade in Canada, immigrant-serving organizations have a variety of programs. Some give workshops on job search skills, where participants get an overview of the job market where they live. Participants learn among other things, how to write a good résumé and how to behave in an interview. In some areas, there are job-finding clubs, mentoring programs, programs to help you get volunteer work experience, and wage subsidy programs.

- **Your personal "network":** One of the best ways to learn about jobs is to talk to people. They can be people you know well, or people you have just met. Even if they cannot lead you directly to a job, they can provide you with information, ideas and names of other people who might be able to help and encourage you.

- **The Internet:** Many Web sites have information on job opportunities. You can search for a job on-line in any part of Canada. Some sites also give practical advice on how to plan your job search. Others allow you to apply for a job directly on the Internet, or to post your résumé (in English or French). When you do this, your résumé goes into a database that can be searched by employers. Try visiting the following Web sites, run by the federal government:

- **www.hrdc-drhc.gc.ca:** This is the national Web site of Human Resources Development Canada, a federal department. It is also the gateway to many of the sites mentioned below.

- **ele-spe.hrdc-drhc.gc.ca:** This is an on-line database of jobs and work or business opportunities across Canada. It matches work to people and people to work. You can click on the province where you plan to settle and submit a list of your skills to the database to find work opportunities that match your profile.

- **worksearch.gc.ca:** This site will take you through all the steps needed to choose a career and to carry out an effective work search.

- **www.workinfonet.ca:** This is a national site for career and labour market information. It will link you to job information for each province and territory. It also includes information on self employment, education and training.

- **jb-ge.hrdc-drhc.gc.ca:** This is the "Job Bank" Web site. It contains an on-line database of thousands of job vacancies across Canada.

- **lmi-imt.hrdc-drhc.gc.ca:** This site will link you to detailed labour market information for every city in Canada.

- **www.SkillNet.ca:** This is a large network of job and career information Web sites. It can link you to full-time and part-time job opportunities.

- **www.canadait.com:** This site is a gateway to job opportunities in the information technology and communications sector. It has links to company directories and associations that will help you find potential employers.

- **www.jobs.gc.ca:** This site posts federal government jobs available across the country and accepts on-line applications.

- **www.integration-net.cic.gc.ca:** This site is run by Citizenship and Immigration Canada. It includes links to many different types of jobs and other useful information for newcomers.

> TIP ! When you arrive in Canada, refer to the pamphlet called "Finding Help in Your Community" in the booklet *Welcome to Canada: What You Should Know* for a list of the immigrant-serving organizations across Canada. Contact an agency in your area and ask about job search programs for newcomers.

Employment laws

Federal and provincial laws protect workers and employers by setting minimum wage levels, health and safety standards, and hours of work. They provide for maternity leave, annual paid vacation and protection of children who are working. There are also human rights laws that protect employees from unfair treatment by employers based on sex, age, race, religion or disability.

Discrimination

There are laws to protect workers from discrimination. For example, an employer must hire employees on the basis of their qualifications. Employers cannot refuse to hire you because they don't like your skin colour or your religion. This is discrimination. It is also discrimination if you are refused a job because of your age, sex, marital status, disability or sexual orientation.

DEDUCTIONS AND TAXABLE BENEFITS

Whether you are a Canadian citizen or a permanent resident, when you are hired, your employer will deduct money from your pay cheque to pay for the following:

Income tax

All Canadian residents who are old enough to work must file an income tax return each year, whether they earned any money or not. That is the law. If you are working for an employer, a percentage of your pay cheque will be deducted and sent to the federal government to cover the income tax that you owe. If too much is deducted, you will get a refund. If you paid too little, you will have to pay more. This money helps pay the cost of government services.

Canada Pension Plan

A small part of your pay cheque goes into this plan. When you retire, you will receive a monthly pension from the federal government. The amount will vary according to how many years you worked in Canada before retiring and what your salary was. Residents of Quebec pay into the Quebec Pension Plan, which works the same way as the federal plan. These plans also include survivor's pensions for the spouses of deceased pensioners, disability pensions and death benefits.

Employment Insurance

When you are working, a small percentage of your pay cheque will be deducted each month to go into the Employment Insurance Account. Your employer contributes to the account as well. Employment Insurance gives money to eligible, unemployed Canadian residents for a short time, while they look for a new job or take some training to learn new skills.

Taxable benefits

Your employer may provide some benefits (for example, life insurance, special medical care, a dental plan or a private pension plan) that are taxable.

Union dues

If you are in a union, and the union has an agreement with your employer, some money will be deducted to pay for the union dues.

GENERAL INFORMATIONABOUT CANADA

- **Geography**
- **Distances**
- **Population**
- **Map of Canada**
- **The Francophone population**
- **History**
- **Economy**
- **Government**
- **Federal government**
- **Provincial governments**
- **Territorial governments**
- **Municipal governments**
- **Bilingualism**
- **Multiculturalism**
- **Protecting the environment -- Sustainable development**

Geography

Canada consists of 10 provinces and three territories in five main regions the Atlantic region, Central Canada, the Prairies, the West Coast and the North. The culture and population are different in each region.

The **Atlantic** region consists of the provinces of Nova Scotia, New Brunswick, Prince Edward Island, and Newfoundland and Labrador Activities such as fishing, farming, forestry, tourism and mining are important to the Atlantic economy.

Central Canada consists of the provinces of Ontario and Quebec. This is the most populated region of the country. Together, Ontario and Quebec produce more than three-quarters of all Canadian manufactured goods.

The **Prairies** include the provinces of Manitoba, Saskatchewan and Alberta. Much of the land is flat and fertile, excellent for farming and rich in energy resources. In western Alberta, the Prairies end and the Rocky Mountains begin. The Canadian Rockies include some of the largest peaks in North America.

On the **West Coast,** the province of British Columbia is famous for its mountain ranges and forests. Natural resources such as lumber and fish are important to the economy. Fruit farming is also a major industry, as is tourism.

The **North** consists of Canada's three territories: Yukon, the Northwest Territories and Nunavut. Together, they make up over one-third of Canada's land mass. Northern resources include oil, natural gas, gold, lead and zinc.

Distances

Distances in Canada are measured in kilometres. Canada is over 7,000 kilometres from east to west. You would need seven days to drive from Halifax, Nova Scotia, to Vancouver, British Columbia. By airplane, the same trip would take about seven hours.

Population

Canada has about 31 million people. More than 80 percent of all the people in Canada live in towns and cities within 250 kilometres of the United States border. Ottawa is Canada's capital city, with a population of nearly one million. It is located in the province of Ontario. Canada's largest cities are Toronto, Ontario (4.4 million people); Montréal, Quebec (3.4 million); and Vancouver, British Columbia (1.9 million).

Map of Canada

Region
Province/Territory
Capital

Atlantic Region
Newfoundland and Labrador
St. John's

Prince Edward Island
Charlottetown

Nova Scotia
Halifax

New Brunswick
Fredericton

Central Canada
Quebec
Québec

Ontario
Toronto

Prairie Provinces
Manitoba
Winnipeg

Saskatchewan
Regina

Alberta
Edmonton

West Coast
British Columbia
Victoria

North
Nunavut
Iqaluit

Northwest Territories
Yellowknife

Yukon
Whitehorse

Note: *You can view a full size coloured North American map by visiting following link.*

http://atlas.gc.ca/site/english/archives/5th_edition/mcrp85/archivemap_view_bigimage

The Francophone Population

French is the mother tongue of 6.6 million Canadians. Most Francophones live in Quebec, but almost one million Francophones live in Canada's other provinces and territories. About 76 percent of Francophones living outside Quebec live in Ontario and New Brunswick. Manitoba, Alberta and British Columbia each have approximately 50,000 Francophones, while Nova Scotia has 35,000 and Saskatchewan has fewer than 20,000. The areas with the smallest French-speaking populations are Prince Edward Island, Newfoundland and Labrador, and the three territories.

TIP ! For information on Francophone communities outside Quebec, visit the following Web sites: franco.ca/atlas/ or www.ocol-clo.gc.ca/7e_2.htm

History

Canada is a land of many cultures and many peoples. Aboriginal peoples have occupied the territory now called Canada for several thousands of years. Everybody else, either by birth or by descent, has been an immigrant -- we have all come from somewhere else. It has been said that Canada is a "nation of immigrants."

There are three main groups of Aboriginal peoples in Canada: the First Nations, the Inuit and the Métis. There are more than 50 different languages spoken by Canada's Aboriginal peoples, most of which are spoken only in Canada. In fact, the name "Canada" may have come from the word "Kanata," which means a settlement in the language of the Huron-Iroquois

First Nations peoples.

As a country, Canada came into being on July 1, 1867. This event is known as "Confederation." Before 1867, the French arrived first, then the British. Each brought their own language, system of government, laws and culture. In 1763, after a long war between the British and the French, all of Canada came under British rule and was known as "British North America."

In the late 18th and into the 19th century, during and after the time of the American Revolution, many African-Americans and United Empire Loyalists fled the United States for Canada, where British ties remained and slavery had been abolished.

During the mid- to late 19th and early 20th century, waves of immigrants arrived from Europe, attracted by the opportunity of a new and better life in Canada. Some settled in towns and cities; others worked in factories, mines and lumber camps. Many were farmers who turned the Prairie region into wheat fields. Asian immigrants from China, Japan and India settled mainly in the western provinces during this time. Many immigrants helped build Canada's national railways, which joined the east and west coasts and opened up the interior for settlement.

After both world wars, thousands of Europeans came to Canada as immigrants and refugees and helped build Canada's post-war economy. Canada's experience during and after the Second World War raised awareness of the needs of refugees and the desire of families to be together.

Over the last 50 years, people from all over the globe have sought a better life or have sought refuge in Canada, fleeing civil wars, political unrest and natural disasters.

Canada still needs the skills, talents and enthusiasm of newcomers to build our country, together with those who have come before them. All of this has been reflected in Canada's immigration and refugee policies. Today, Canada is home to immigrants from more than 240 countries. Most newcomers decide to become citizens of Canada, after they are settled and have met the requirements of Canadian citizenship.

Economy

Canada has a diversified economy. Natural resources industries, such as forestry, mining, oil and gas extraction, farming and fishing, are important sources of jobs and export earnings. Canada is also a world leader in the fields of telecommunications, biotechnology, aerospace technologies and pharmaceuticals. More and more jobs involve work in service industries or in information technology. Along with the United States and Mexico, Canada is a partner in the North American Free Trade Agreement.

Canada has a decimal system of currency. The Canadian dollar is the basic unit of money. The most common paper bills are the $5, $10 and $20, but $50 and $100 bills are also used. Canadian coins include the penny (one cent), nickel (five cents), dime (10 cents), quarter (25 cents), loonie ($1) and toonie ($2).

Government

Canada is a federation, with a parliamentary system of government. Being a federation means that powers and responsibilities are divided between the federal government and the 10 provincial governments. Canada also has three territorial jurisdictions. Canada has three levels of government: federal, provincial and municipal (cities and towns). These governments are elected by the citizens of Canada.

Federal government (Government of Canada)

The federal government is responsible for:

- defence;

- foreign policy and foreign relations;
- banking;
- the postal service;
- criminal law;
- immigration; and
- citizenship.

Provincial governments

Provincial governments are responsible for:

- education; and
- municipal institutions.

They also share responsibility with the federal government for:

- health services;
- farming;
- social assistance;
- transportation; and
- the environment.

Territorial Governments

The Northwest Territories, Yukon and Nunavut are not sovereign units. They get their powers from the federal parliament, but they have elected assemblies that follow many of the same practices as the provincial governments.

Municipal Governments

Municipal governments have functions delegated to them by other levels of government. They are responsible for local matters and services. These include:

- police and fire protection;
- water and sewer services;
- recreation; and
- local public transportation.

If you are interested, the Web site **canada.gc.ca/howgoc/glance_e.html** has more information about how Canadians govern themselves.

Bilingualism

Under the *Official Languages Act,* Canada is an officially bilingual country. This means that Canadians have the right to get federal government services in English or French, no matter what part of Canada they are living in.

New Brunswick is the only province that is officially bilingual. New Brunswick residents receive services in both official languages from all of their provincial government departments and agencies.

In Quebec, French is the official language and in most cases, provincial and municipal services are provided in French.

In the other provinces and territories, English is the official language, and the availability of provincial services in both official languages varies.

At the municipal level, the availability of services in both official languages varies greatly.

Multiculturalism

Canada is populated by people who have come from every part of the world. Through the *Canadian Multiculturalism Act,* the government encourages Canadians to take pride in their language, religion and heritage and to keep their customs and traditions, as long as they don't break Canadian laws.

Protecting the environment --Sustainable development

Canada has a beautiful natural environment. Because we have lots of land and a small population, most of our country is wild and unspoiled. However, it is becoming harder to preserve our environment as our population and cities grow. Pollution helps cause large-scale environmental problems, such as acid rain. And as more people use and live in natural areas, threats to the environment increase.

Canadians are very concerned about environmental issues. They know that damage to the environment can be hard to fix.

Canadians know that economic growth is crucial for the future prosperity of Canada. But growth must be managed carefully so that it does not harm the environment. The Canadian government is committed to "sustainable development," which is economic growth that does not hurt the environment and helps people.

A healthy environment is important to quality of life. Everyone living in Canada should act in a responsible way, both toward the environment and within their community. This way, future Canadians have the opportunity to live in a country that is clean and prosperous. Both individuals and groups can help Canada develop in a sustainable way.

Here are a few things you can do to help protect quality of life:

- throw waste paper and other garbage in public garbage cans;

- compost, recycle and re-use as many products as possible, such as paper, glass and cans;

153

- conserve energy and water by turning off lights and taps when you are not using them;

- walk, join a car pool, or use a bicycle or public transit whenever possible;

- use products that are environmentally friendly;

- plant trees or grow a garden, but avoid using chemicals;

- never pour paint, oil or other harmful chemicals down sinks or toilets, into sewers or onto the ground (telephone your local government to find out where you can throw out these hazardous materials);

- volunteer with a local organization; and

- educate yourself and your children about environmental issues.

For further information, contact:

Environment Canada
Enquiry Centre
351 St. Joseph Boulevard
Hull, Quebec K1A 0H3

Telephone: 1 (819) 997-2800
1 800 668-6767 (toll-free, within Canada)

Fax: 1 (819) 953-2225
E-mail: enviroinfo@ec.gc.ca
Web site: **www.ec.gc.ca**

TIP ! Contact your local government to find out about the services and bylaws that protect the environment (for example, garbage disposal schedules, water management and recycling programs). You can find local government telephone numbers in the Blue Pages of the telephone book.

THE CANADIAN WAY OF LIFE

- Family life and family law
- Marriage, divorce and the law
- Birth control and family planning
- Youth and their parents
- Youth and the law
- Standards and expectations
  - o Important social standards
- Some Canadian laws
- Interacting with officials
  - o People in authority
  - o Public officials
  - o Police officers

Family Life And Family Law

Many people in Canada find that it takes two incomes to raise a family, even though parents are having fewer children. Most mothers have a job outside the home, and in many families, both parents share the work of shopping, cooking, cleaning the house and looking after the children. Because divorce has become more common, there are many one-parent families in Canada. Most single parents who raise their children on a full-time basis are women. There are also same-sex couples with children.

Marriage, divorce and the law

Canadian law views marriage as a legal agreement or contract between a man and a woman. Married people are considered equal partners. Marriage laws apply to all Canadian citizens and permanent residents. Many unmarried couples live together. In most provinces, unmarried heterosexual couples who have lived together for a certain period of time have legal status as "common-law" couples. They may call each other "husband" and "wife," or they may simply say "my partner."

Either the wife or the husband can ask for a divorce. This request will normally be approved by the courts if both people have agreed to end the marriage. Divorce will also be approved if one partner has been harmed through cruelty, adultery or a similar injustice.

Birth control and family planning

Many people use birth control. It is a matter of personal choice. Women can get a prescription for birth control pills from a doctor. Family planning information is available from government departments of health and public health offices, as well as from local health clinics. Abortion is legal but is only available from a doctor.

Youth and their parents

When children arrive in Canada, they usually learn about Canadian life quickly through schools, television, movies and music. If they need to learn English or French, they often learn it quite quickly.

Parents find out about Canadian life differently, as they search for housing and work. They too may need to learn English or French, but often need more time than their children to do so.

If you have children, you will know that you see the world somewhat differently than they do, because you are older and have more life experience. After immigrating to Canada, however, you may find that these differences increase, because you are having different experiences of Canadian life. These differences affect the behaviour of all family members and can lead to tension in the family between parents and their children.

Discussing concerns with teachers, doctors, public health workers, social workers, settlement workers, and friends and relatives who have already settled in Canada will help you and your children understand your experiences and make good choices about your future.

Youth and the law

Youth in Canada who commit a crime are held accountable for their actions. However they are not dealt with in the same way as adult offenders. This is because they may not have an adult's understanding of their crime. They are also more likely than adult offenders to be reformed and become law-abiding citizens. The law for young offenders is called the *Youth Criminal Justice Act.*

STANDARDS AND EXPECTATIONS

Some of Canada's standards for public behaviour may be more conservative than you are used to, while others may seem more liberal. For example, Canadians may seem impersonal and cold to some newcomers; to others, we may seem overly friendly.

Important social standards

Social practices -- not laws -- govern many types of behaviour in Canada. Some traditions are well established and are politely but firmly enforced. For example:

- **Lining up, or queuing:** People normally line up or queue according to the principle of "first-come, first-served." They will be angry if you push ahead in a line-up instead of waiting your turn.

- **Not smoking in private homes:** Most Canadians do not smoke. When you are in people's homes, you should always ask their permission to smoke. If they do not smoke themselves, they may ask you to go outside to smoke.

- **Being on time:** You should always arrive on time -- at school, at work and for any meeting. People who are often late may be fired from their jobs or suspended from school. Many Canadians will not wait more than 10 or 15 minutes for someone who has a business meeting. For social events, people expect that you will arrive within half an hour of the stated time.

- **Respect for the environment:** Canadians respect the natural environment and expect people to avoid littering (dropping waste paper and other garbage on the street or throwing it out of your car). They will expect you to carry your garbage until you can find a proper garbage can.

- **Bargaining:** Bargaining for a better price is not common in Canada but there are some exceptions. For example, almost everyone bargains for a better price when buying a car or a house, or other expensive items such as furniture. People who sell things privately may also bargain.

- **Smart shopping:** Stores compete with one another to attract customers, so it is wise to check and compare prices at different stores before you buy. **Note:** The price marked on goods in stores does not usually include the federal and provincial sales taxes which add from 7 percent to 15 percent to the cost of an item depending on the province in which you buy it.

> **TIP !** If you have questions about social standards or customs, you can ask the local immigrant-serving organization for advice. If you have been matched with a Canadian family under the Host Program, the family members can help answer your questions as well.

SOME CANADIAN LAWS

Some laws you should be aware of

- It is illegal to drive without a driver's licence, registration and insurance.

- It is illegal to drive if you have been drinking alcohol.

- The driver and all passengers must wear seat belts at all times when driving in Canada.

- Babies and children who are too small to wear seat belts must be placed in properly installed infant or child car seats, appropriate to the age and weight of the child.

- Children under 12 years of age cannot be left at home alone, or to care for younger children.

- All children aged six to 16 must attend school.

- Smoking is not permitted in federal buildings, in elevators, on Canadian airlines, on buses and on other public transportation, nor in many banks, shops, restaurants and other public places (some municipalities have banned smoking in all public buildings).

- Depending on which part of Canada you live in, you must be either 18 or 19 years old to buy or drink alcohol in any form.

- It is against the law to hit your spouse or children, either in the home or in public.

- It is illegal to use, buy or sell marijuana, heroin, cocaine and other addictive drugs.

- It is illegal to make any kind of sexual remarks or advances if the other person does not like them.

INTERACTING WITH OFFICIALS

Knowing how to behave and what to expect can be very useful when you are dealing with public officials and people in authority. Usually, there is no need to worry about making mistakes. Except for matters of law, most Canadians do not insist on strict formality. Officials who know that you are a newcomer will make allowances for your inexperience with Canadian ways.

People in authority

In Canada, a person's authority is related to his or her position and responsibility. Women hold the same kinds of positions as men and have the same kinds of authority. People do not have authority just because of their name, status, social class or sex.

Public officials

Public officials will normally treat you in a polite but impersonal way. Public officials follow set procedures. They do not make the rules. They may not want to or be able to become involved with your situation. Do not respond to them in a personal or emotional way. Never try to bribe a public official. Bribery and other forms of corruption are illegal and will offend most Canadians.

Police Officers

The police are part of the community and are accountable to the public. They may be either men or women. They are trained to serve and protect the public, including you. Police operate within strict regulations and follow established procedures. Canadians expect honesty and fairness from the police.

Calling the police: Most cities and towns have an emergency number for the police. Call this number if you or someone else is hurt or in danger, or if you see a crime taking place. In most parts of Canada, the emergency number is 911. Emergency numbers are always printed inside the front cover of the telephone book.

What if you are questioned by a police officer?

- Call the police officer "officer."
- Accept the police officer's authority; do not try to argue.
- Be ready to show identification if a police officer asks you for it. If you are stopped by the police while driving a car, the officer will probably ask you for your driver's licence, proof of insurance and car registration.
- Tell the officer the facts about what has happened. Do not offer your own opinion.
- Never try to give money to a police officer. Canadians do not bribe police officers. It is a serious crime to do this.

What if you are arrested by a police officer?

- Police officers must tell you who they are and show you their badge number.
- They must explain why they are arresting you and tell you what your rights are.

- They must allow you to call a lawyer right away. If you don't have a lawyer, they must give you the Legal Aid telephone number and let you call.

- You do not have to give any information, other than your name and address, until you have talked to a lawyer.

YOUR RIGHTS AND OBLIGATIONS

- **Personal rights and freedoms**
- **Children's rights**
- **Women's rights**
- **Senior citizens' rights**
- **Becoming a Canadian citizen**
- **Responsible and active citizenship**

As a newcomer, you should be aware of your rights and obligations. Having the right to participate in Canadian society also means that you have a responsibility to respect the rights and freedoms of others and to obey Canada's laws.

Personal rights and freedoms

The *Canadian Charter of Rights and Freedoms* describes the basic principles and values by which Canadians live. The Charter is part of Canada's Constitution. The Charter protects you from the moment you arrive on Canadian soil. It gives everyone in Canada the following fundamental rights and freedoms:

- the right to life, liberty and personal security;
- freedom of conscience and religion;
- freedom of thought, belief, opinion and expression, including freedom of the press and other media of communication;
- freedom to hold peaceful meetings;

- freedom to join groups;
- the right to live and work anywhere in Canada;
- protection from unreasonable search or seizure and arbitrary detainment and imprisonment;
- the right to be presumed innocent until proven guilty;
- the right to have a lawyer;
- the right to a fair trial, through due process of law; and
- the right to equal protection and benefit under the law, without discrimination.

Children's Rights

In Canada, you are required by law to properly care for your children. Police, doctors, teachers and children's aid officials will act when children are being abused. This includes any form of harm and abuse -- physical, psychological or sexual. All forms of child abuse are serious crimes. In serious cases of abuse, children can be taken away from their parents.

Physical abuse is any intentional physical contact that causes injury. For example, spanking a child long enough or hard enough to cause bruises, or spanking with anything other than an open hand, is a form of abuse. Some cultural practices, such as female circumcision, are also considered physical abuse and are against the law.

Psychological abuse includes terror and humiliation.

Sexual abuse includes any form of sexual contact between an adult and a child.

Neglect is also a form of child abuse. Parents who fail to protect and provide for their children are guilty of neglect. By law, children **under 12 cannot be left alone to look after themselves or younger siblings.**

Kids' "help-lines" are available for children who need someone to help them or just need someone to talk to.

Women's rights

In Canada, women have the same legal status, rights and opportunities as men. Most Canadian men respect women as equals -- socially, in the workplace and in the home. Violence against women is against the law. Women who are abused can seek help for themselves and their children in local shelters. They are also entitled to legal protection to keep them safe.

Senior citizens' rights

A senior citizen is someone 65 years of age or older. It is common in Canadian society for healthy senior citizens to live on their own, instead of living with their children. Older people who need special care often move to a retirement or nursing home that provides trained staff and health-care workers. However, many Canadians still care for older family members in their own home.

Old Age Security: The Old Age Security (OAS) program ensures a basic income to all people in Canada 65 years of age or over who meet the residence requirements. Usually, OAS is paid after a person has lived in Canada at least 10 years, although people who have lived or worked in countries with which Canada has an agreement may qualify after as little as one year. Low-income people who get OAS may also qualify for the Guaranteed Income Supplement (GIS) and their spouses (or widows) may also qualify for the Spouse's Allowance if they are between 60 and 64 years of age.

The Canada Pension Plan pays benefits to contributors in the event of retirement or disability, as well as benefits to surviving spouses and orphans in the event of death of a contributor. All workers in Canada contribute to the plan.

> **TIP !** You may also be eligible for old age security benefits from your former country.

Becoming A Canadian Citizen

Once you have been in Canada for at least three years, you may apply to become a Canadian citizen. Immigrants who become citizens have the same rights as citizens who were born in Canada. As a citizen you can:

- vote and be a candidate for political office in federal, provincial and territorial elections;
- apply for a Canadian passport;
- enter and leave Canada freely;
- enjoy full economic rights, including the right to own any type of property; and
- be eligible for some pension benefits.

An adult applying for Canadian citizenship must:

- be at least 18 years old;
- be a permanent resident of Canada who entered the country legally;
- have lived in Canada for three of the four years before applying for citizenship;
- speak either English or French;
- know something about Canada's history, geography, system of government and voting;
- know the rights and responsibilities of citizenship;
- apply for citizenship and pass the citizenship test; and
- take the oath of citizenship.

You cannot become a Canadian citizen if you:

- are considered a risk to Canada's security;
- are under a deportation order;
- are in prison, on parole from prison or on probation; or
- have been found guilty of a serious crime within the past three years.

Responsible and active citizenship

For many Canadians, being a good citizen means getting involved in their community. Regardless of your interests, contributing to your society is rewarding and is appreciated by others who, like you, are proud to make Canada their home.

> **TIP !** Getting involved in volunteer activities is also an excellent way to meet new people, make friends, practise English or French, and learn about Canadian customs.

AFTERWORD

We hope this information has answered some of your questions about Canada, about adapting to life in Canada and about the Canadian way of life. As you prepare to leave for Canada, refer again to the tips and checklists provided here.

One last checklist:

- Have you gathered all of your essential and important documents? Have you had them translated into English or French?
- Have you considered buying health insurance for the time you are traveling and for the short period before you become eligible for Canada's Medicare system?
- Do you know what you can and cannot bring into Canada?
- Have you prepared yourself for finding work in Canada?
- Have you researched Canada's labour market in general and in each of the five regions? Have you used the Internet to learn about finding work in Canada?
- Have you considered living in one of Canada's smaller or medium-sized cities, or in a rural community? Have you used the Internet to learn about these choices?
- Have you considered the season and climate you will find when you arrive, and the clothing that you will need?
- Have you considered contacting an immigrant-serving organization soon after you arrive in Canada?
- Have you considered taking English or French lessons through the LINC (Language Instruction for Newcomers to Canada) program?

The best way to adjust to your new home will be to get involved! Try to speak English or French as much as possible, even if you make mistakes. Ask questions when you need help. Most people are pleased to help and will understand your needs. With time, you will feel more and more at home. Canada and Canadians will welcome you and your family into the larger Canadian family. Good luck on your journey!

Welcome to Canada -- your new home

UNDERSTANDING CULTURAL SHOCK

1.   WHAT IS CULTURE SHOCK?

It happens when a person is placed in a different social setting. The accepted social rules are not immediately clear and one does not know what is expected, or how to get things done. Move from one country to another or one culture to another is a perfect example; however, culture shock also occurs to people within their own country. For example:

- Moving from the countryside to a large city,
- Moving from one region to another,
- Joining the military and experiencing "boot camp",
- Changing schools or jobs;

You can, no doubt, think of others.

What do you do in such situations? Observe, seek advice from others, begin to follow the leads of others, build your confidence and then begin to participate fully. There are well designed set of actions which you can use to minimize culture shock and make a successful transition to your new or overseas situation.

Whenever a person enters a strange culture, many of the familiar cues which have been a part of his everyday experiences are removed. He may feel like a fish out of water. He has come face to face with a problem we call "culture shock". Oberg, a prominent social scientist, states that "culture shock is precipitated by the anxiety that results from losing all familiar sings and symbols of social intercourse. These signs or cues include the thousand and one ways in which people orientate themselves to the situation of daily life". The term culture shock describes how our mind tells us to act when we are in a new and different environment.

Culture shock affects everyone – it will affect you. Some people are affected slightly and quickly adjust, whilst others receive a severe shock and never really enjoy their overseas experiences. Basically, culture shock is a mental attitude problem which affects people soon after arrival in the foreign environment.

Culture shock seems to affect wives more than husbands. Usually, the husband has his profession and job-related activities to occupy his time, but the wife is the one who must cope with the rigors of the new environment. The strain on her is the greatest. She must adapt her methods and activities to provide a stabilizing influence for her entire family.

The chart included in this article depict the various phases of culture shock. As can be seen, shortly after the family has arrived in the foreign environment, the "honeymoon" is over and realization sets in. Some people develop a mild culture shock and adjust easily to the environment, while others remain in a depressed state for their entire overseas tour. This crisis phase is very real for many people and may easily prevail for several months. An adjustment and recovery phase follows this crisis phase as the individual adjusts to his new environment. Five or six months after arrival, most individuals have adjusted adequately and are actively pursuing their own interests and activities.

2.   HOW TO OVERCOME CULTURE SHOCK

Realizing that you will experience culture shock is half the battle of overcoming it. Accept the fact that the adjustment and transition into the new environment is difficult, but remember that the situation is temporary and will pass as you learn the language, mannerisms and local customs. When you find yourself getting angry, 'uptight' and condemning everyone around you, realize that you are under an emotional strain and that you will be adjusting to the unfamiliar situation. Culture shock seems to build up until it overpowers you. It results from a series of little things which are hard to put your finger on.

The following suggestions are offered to help in overcoming culture shock:

A.   Make a conscious effort to get to know the people of the host country. Learn as much as you can about the language, history and the culture.

B.   Recognize that your negative attitude and reactions are caused by culture shock.

C.   Consciously look for logical reasons behind the customs and activities you identify as being different from your own. Accentuate the positive and look for the good traits and characteristics of the foreign environment.

D.   Identify a host country national or some other person to whom you would enjoy talking about your feelings and situation. That means a friend.

E.   Keep a diary of your thoughts and feelings. Every few weeks review what you have written and reflect back on your thoughts and feelings.

F.   Develop some useful hobbies and outside interests to occupy some of your spare time. Don't sit around complaining about how miserable you are.

G.   Be flexible, curious and self-reliant. Make the most out of a seemingly unhappy situation.

H.   Remember, you are not alone. Others are having the same problems, although they might not be willing to admit it.

After you adjustment phase is completed, you will undoubtedly associate with others who are going through the trials of culture shock. Remember how you felt in your crisis phase. Be patient, understanding and sympathetic. Soon, time which is the great healer, will set things right.

3.   CULTURE SHOCK VICTIMS – WHO ARE THEY?

Probably every person relocating to a new culture suffers varying degrees of this psychological malady. Do not think this problem applies to only Eastern going to Western countries, it even happens to others nationals going to Eastern countries. Having culture shock does not indicate a psychological weakness or the inability to adjust to your new environment. Experiencing culture shock is probably a necessary phase of making a successful transition. The keys to overcoming culture shock are:

-     Knowing that you may encounter it;
-     Understanding that it is normal and part of your adjustment;
-     Recognizing the symptoms, if they occur;
-     Taking a logical and practical approach to conquering it.

4.   ORIGIN AND DEVELOPMENT

Culture shock is a psychological malady that has been responsible for much of the personnel turnover experienced by Immigrants arriving in Canada. It occurs when people suddenly find themselves in an unfamiliar environment. The origin of the shock is in the anxiety resulting from the absence of familiar signs and symbols of one's basic culture. Each person's peace of mind, emotional balance and efficiency depend on hundreds of cues instilled in the mind whilst growing up in a specific culture. In response to these cues we form habits that are learned whilst confronting situations of daily life. These include when to smile, laugh, shake hands and courtesies such as ladies first, queuing up and many more expressions that reveal how we think, how we feel and what we believe.

When a person enters a different culture environment, all or most of his life patterns are absent. He can become like the proverbial "fish out of water".

5.   COMMON CULTURE SHOCK SYMPTOMS

Each person may exhibit different symptoms and varying degrees of culture shock and may possibly exhibit some of the following:

-     A verbal rejection of the new country.

- Unwarranted criticism of the culture and the people.
- Constant complaints about the climate.
- Utopian ideas concerning one's native culture.
- A viewpoint that all things from the past are suddenly wonderful.
- Making light of, or forgetting serious past misfortunes and problems.
- Excessive washing of the hands.
- Continuous concern over the purity of the drinking water.
- Unreasonable concern about the food to be eaten.
- Fear of touching or physical contact with the local people.
- Inappropriate anger over slight delays and frustrations.
- Refusal to learn the new language.
- Indifference about meeting the local people.
- Pre-occupation with returning home.
- Pre-occupation with the fear of being robbed, cheated or molested.
- Pressing desire to talk with people who really make sense.
- Misconception of the local's attitude towards a foreigner.
- Expression of other non-valid criticism.

6.   POST CULTURE SHOCK

Even the individual who remains in the country and adapts his lifestyle to the local donations of everyday life, will continually encounter the need to adjust to such factors as:

- Social custom
- Language
- Job search
- Domestic help
- Housing
- Shopping
- Traffic
- Climate
- Unfamiliar sights and sounds.

The locals will try to help, but they do not always seem to understand the newcomer's great concern over these insignificant frustrations, many of which they have grown up with. Consequently, they may be perceived as being insensitive and indifferent.

If the person suffering from culture shock is upset and shows anger, the locals may sense this hostility and will probably either avoid him or respond in a similar manner, consequently compounding the problem.

7. CULTURE SHOCK RESULTS

The end result, whether positive or negative, depends entirely upon how you handle the situation. The Immigrants who adjusts and adapts to the new environment becomes a happier and more productive thus settles in considerably short period of time.

The Immigrants who becomes discontented and directs their displeasures towards others, causing friction within the community, is usually decide to go back to home country and may retain a bitter attitude towards all foreign countries and their nationals.

GENERAL STAGES OF CULTURE SHOCK

	PRE-DEPARTURE	FIRST MONTH (Exploratory or Honeymoon)	2ND & 3RD MONTH (Crisis)	4TH & 5TH MONTH (Adjustments)	SIXTH MONTH (Recovery & Equilibrium)
GENERAL ATTITUDES	Excitement & pleasure	Fascination Spirit of Adventure	Disenchanted Restless and Impatient	Gradual Recovery and Adjustment	Normal
SIGNIFICANT EVENTS	Planning, Packing, Processing, Partying, Parting	Red Carpet Welcome, New Office, New friends, Colleagues and Living Quarters (Others stand as buffers between the new family and the problems)	**Varied** - Fully Duty Responsibilities - Shipment delayed - Smells, Foods, and Local travel. Complications	**Varied** Acceptable Duty performance	Normal Duty Performance.
EMOTIONAL RESPONSE TO EVENTS	Excitement and Enthusiasm. - Some concern about leaving friends, family and the familiar environment.	Tourist Enthusiasm.	Insecure and Irritable. - Home sickness. - Mental fatigue	Sparking Interest. - Lessening of tension. - Return of a sense of humour - Empathy for others.	Emotional Equilibrium. - Enjoyment.
ATTITUTINAL RESPONSE TO EVENTS	Anticipation	Curiosity and enthusiasm. - Job enthusiasm. - High expectations	Frustration, Withdrawn and antagonistic. - Skepticism and uncertainly. - Questions the values of people, self and job -	Emerging. - Constructive attitude. - Understanding of own feelings and cultural patterns.	Equilibrium .
PHYSICAL RESPONSES TO EVENTS	Weary, but normal health	Minor insomnia, slight headaches.	Minor illness	Normal health	Normal health.

WORKING IN CANADA

Finding employment in Canada requires planning. You should learn as much as possible before you apply to immigrate. Be aware that there is no guarantee that you will find a job and be able to work in your preferred occupation.

Regulated and Non-Regulated Occupations

Some professions and trades are regulated in Canada to protect public health and safety. Twenty percent of people working in Canada, such as nurses, engineers, electricians and teachers, work in regulated occupations

Provincial and territorial organizations are responsible for:

- setting entry requirements for people in individual occupations;
- recognizing credentials, training or experience; and
- issuing licences required to work in regulated occupations.

The way to have your qualifications recognized is different in each province and territory, and for each occupation. In most cases, you can only apply to have your qualifications recognized once you are in Canada. You may be asked to:

- provide documentation of qualifications;
- take a language test;
- complete a technical exam (with applicable fee); and
- do supervised work.

Non-regulated Occupations

If your occupation is **not** regulated, you do not need a licence. You employer will decide what requirements you must meet and if you need to register with a professional association.

For more information on regulated and non-regulated occupations in Canada:

174

- Canadian Information Centre for International Credentials
- Work Destinations at Human Resources Development Canada.
- Workopolis

Information for foreign-trained medical doctors

Information on requirements to practise

Those who practise this profession use one of the following titles: doctor, medical doctor, physician, family physician, general practitioner, or resident-in-training for one of these roles. Entry into the professions is **regulated** in Canada. This means that the requirements to practise are set by each provincial and territorial medical association. Once you know where you will settle and work in Canada, contact the appropriate provincial/territorial medical association (see list below) to obtain further information.

Information for Graduates of Foreign Medical Schools

If you immigrate to Canada through the Family Class or Refugee categories without regard to occupation, you must sign a statement that you have been fully informed of the difficulties you will encounter in obtaining a licence to practise medicine.

Before your application for immigration can be approved, your basic medical knowledge must be evaluated. In most cases, this means that you must pass the Medical Council of Canada's Evaluating Examination (MCCEE). This examination evaluates your general medical knowledge compared to that of graduates of Canadian medical schools. It tests your understanding of the principal fields of medicine - including internal medicine, obstetrics and gynecology, pediatrics, psychiatry, preventive medicine and community health, and surgery. Most of the questions are intended to evaluate clinical knowledge, but there are some questions on basic medical sciences.

The examination is held twice yearly, usually in March and September, in various centres in Canada and abroad. It is given in English and in French. Before you are eligible to write the Evaluating Examination, you must complete all the requirements to obtain qualification of Doctor of Medicine, or equivalent, from the university that granted your medical degree.

To obtain an application to write the examination or to receive a list of examination centres, contact the Executive Director at:

Medical Council of Canada (MCC)
P.O. Box 8234, Station T
Ottawa, Ontario K1G 3H7
Canada

Tel.: (613) 521-6012
Fax: (613) 521-9417
http://www.mcc.ca/
Rev. Date: 3/14/2002 6:31:56 PM

Some provinces have pre-residency training for permanent residents of the province who are graduates of foreign medical schools. The contents and length of the program varies in these provinces. For specific details, contact the provincial/territorial licensing authority.

In 2001, only 15.5 per cent of graduates of foreign medical schools who applied to CaRMS were successful in obtaining a postgraduate medical position. Of the 1219 postgraduate training positions in the 2001 match, only 60, or 5 per cent, of the positions were matched to graduates of foreign medical schools.

Information on assessment of qualifications

Contact the Medical Council of Canada for assessment of your qualifications **prior to arrival in Canada.**

Information for foreign-trained engineering technologists and technicians

Information on requirements to practise

In Canada, the different occupations in technology are **not regulated**. In Quebec, the use of the title "technologue professionnel" (professional technologist) is controlled. You do not require certification in order to work as a technician or technologist in the other provinces and the territories. However, certification is available but voluntary in all provinces through the Canadian Council of Technicians and Technologists (CCTT), a federation of the professional associations and societies of technicians and technologists in many applied science and engineering disciplines (see list of disciplines and sub-disciplines at http://www.cctt.ca/dlist.htm).

The provincial associations of CCTT (see list below) handle the certification procedures according to national standards. Once certified as a full member of a provincial association, **technologists** are known either as Certified Engineering Technologists (C.E.T.), Applied Science Technologists (A.Sc.T.), or Registered Engineering Technologists (R.E.T.), depending on the province in which they receive certification and entitlement to the designation. **Technicians** are known as Certified Technicians (C. Tech). In Canada, it is illegal to use these designations without being certified as a full member of an association. In Quebec, membership in the regulatory body is required to use the title of **technologue professionnel/Professional Technologist**, which is a "profession à titre réservé."

The Canadian Technology Accreditation Board (CTAB) evaluates college-level and private programs of study in applied science and engineering technology. The Board includes representatives from the provincial associations and societies, the Department of National Defence (DND), the Canadian Technology Human Resource Board (CTHRB), the Canadian Society for Chemical Technology (CSCT), and the National Council of Deans of Technology (NCDOT). Additional technology educators participate as observers.

Information on assessment of qualifications

For immigration purposes only, the CCTT works with Citizenship and Immigration Canada (CIC) in assessing the qualifications of people applying for permanent residence in Canada who intend to work as technicians or technologists. In this regard, CCTT has prepared an information note entitled Informal Assessment of Foreign Qualifications for Applied Science and Engineering Technicians and Technologists. Note that CCTT charges a fee for this service, and that its assessments do not guarantee recognition of your credentials for purposes of employment or certification in Canada. You may also contact the CCTT for further general information:

Canadian Council of Technicians and Technologists (CCTT)
285 McLeod Street
Ottawa, Ontario K2P 1A1
Canada

Tel.: (613) 238-8123
Fax: (613) 238-8822

Email: ctabadm@magma.ca
http://www.cctt.ca/
Rev. Date: 5/29/2002 10:33:47 AM

The purpose of the CCTT assessment is to evaluate the likelihood of acceptance into the provincial technology association's examination program. As regulatory bodies, the provincial associations are not bound in any way by the candidate's results on the initial immigration assessment. They will conduct their own assessment of certification applicants, for which fees are also charged.

You may also contact an evaluation service, and consult the Fact Sheet No. 2, "Assessment and recognition of credentials for the purpose of employment in Canada." Although the evaluation services offer expert advice on how qualifications obtained abroad compare with credentials obtained in a Canadian province or territory, the evaluation is **advisory only and does not guarantee recognition** of your qualifications for employment or certification purposes in Canada. Please note that they charge a fee for their services.

Information for foreign-trained accountants and auditors

Information on requirements to practise

The occupations of financial auditors and accountants are **regulated** by legislation **in most jurisdictions**. Requirements to practise vary, but membership in a professional accounting association is usually required. The three major national accounting organizations are identified below, and each has its own professional designation: Chartered Accountant (CA), Certified General Accountant (CGA), and Certified Management Accountant (CMA). The related provincial/territorial bodies are listed at the end. Therefore, once you know where you will settle and work in Canada, you should contact the appropriate association for details on licensing procedures.

Canadian Institute of Chartered Accountants (CICA)
227 Wellington Street West
Toronto, Ontario M5V 3H2
Canada

Tel.: (416) 977-3222
Fax: (416) 977-8585

Email: qualification.reform@cica.ca
http://www.cica.ca/
Rev. Date: 3/22/2002 4:59:27 PM

Certified General Accountants Association of Canada (CGA-Canada)
1188 West Georgia Street, Suite 700
Vancouver, British Columbia V6E 4A2
Canada

Tel.: (604) 669-3555 or 1-800-663-1529
Fax: (604) 689-5845

Email: public@cga-canada.org
http://www.cga-canada.org/
Rev. Date: 2/13/2002 10:05:56 AM

Society of Management Accountants of Canada (CMA-Canada)
One Robert Speck Parkway, Suite 1400 P.O. Box 176
Mississauga, Ontario L4Z 3M3
Canada
Tel.: (905) 949-4200 or 1-800-263-7622
Fax: (905) 949-0038

Email: info@cma-canada.org
http://www.cma-canada.org/
Rev. Date: 1/31/2002 11:43:51 AM

Public Accountants

For professional accountants who expect to perform **public accounting services**, particularly as an **auditor** of the financial statements of companies listed on stock exchanges, the requirements for licensure are regulated by legislation as follows:

- **Licences** to practise **public accounting** are **required** by legislation in **Newfoundland, Nova Scotia, Ontario, and Prince Edward Island**. With few exceptions, only CAs are licensed to practise public accounting in Nova Scotia and Ontario. Only CAs may be licensed in Prince Edward Island. Newfoundland legislation provides for the licensing of CAs, CMAs, and CGAs.

- In **Quebec**, the performance of statutory **audits** for publicly listed companies is limited by legislation to CAs. However, CAs, CGAs, and CMAs are able to perform certain other audits in Quebec.

- In **Alberta**, only CAs, CMAs, and CGAs are permitted to engage in **public accounting** if they hold a certificate of practice from one of the three accounting bodies. In British Columbia the right to perform statutory **audits** is restricted to CAs, CGAs, and persons approved by the provincial Auditor Certification Board.

- There is no licensing or certification required by legislation to practise **public accounting** in Manitoba, Saskatchewan, New Brunswick, Northwest Territories, Nunavut, or the Yukon. However, the securities commissions in some of these jurisdictions require that professional accountants performing **audit or review services** for publicly listed companies be CAs, CGAs, or CMAs.

Information for foreign-trained engineers

Information on requirements to practise

The profession of engineer is **regulated** in Canada. It is illegal to practise the profession of engineer or to use the title "engineer" without being licensed as a full member in a provincial or territorial association. **However, individuals can do engineering work under the direct supervision of licensed engineers.**

Provincial and territorial associations of professional engineers are responsible for setting the standards for entry into the profession and for issuing licences to those who meet established standards of qualifications and practice.

Therefore, once you know where you will settle and work in Canada, you should contact the appropriate provincial or territorial association for details on licensure procedures. Below is a <u>list of addresses</u> of the national, provincial, and territorial associations of professional engineers.

List of associations of professional engineers

Alberta

Association of Professional Engineers, Geologists and Geophysicists of Alberta (APEGGA)
10060 Jasper Avenue 1500 Scotia One
Edmonton AB T5J 4A2
Canada

Tel.: (780) 426-3990 or 1-800-661-7020
Fax: (780) 425-1722
http://www.apegga.org/

British Columbia

Association of Professional Engineers and Geoscientists of British Columbia (APEGBC)
200-4010 Regent Street
Burnaby BC V5C 6N2
Canada

Tel.: (604) 430-8035 or 1-888-430-8035
Fax: (604) 430-8085
http://www.apeg.bc.ca/

Manitoba

Association of Professional Engineers and Geoscientists of Manitoba (APEGM)
850A Pembina Highway
Winnipeg MB R3M 2M7
Canada

Tel.: (204) 474-2736
Fax: (204) 474-5960
http://www.apegm.mb.ca/

New Brunswick

Association of Professional Engineers and Geoscientists of New Brunswick (APEGNB)
535 Beaverbrook Court, Suite 105
Fredericton NB E3B 1X6
Canada
Tel.: (506) 458-8083
Fax: (506) 451-9629
http://ctca.unb.ca/apenb/

Newfoundland and Labrador

Association of Professional Engineers and Geoscientists of Newfoundland (APEGN)
10 Fort William Place, Suite 203, P.O. Box 21207
St. John's NF A1A 5B2
Canada

Tel.: (709) 753-7714
Fax: (709) 753-6131
http://www.apegn.nf.ca/

Northwest Territories

Association of Professional Engineers, Geologists and Geophysicists of the Northwest Territories (NAPEGG)
201, 4817-49th Street
Yellowknife NT X1A 3S7
Canada

Tel.: (867) 920-4055
Fax: (867) 873-4058
http://www.napegg.nt.ca/

Nova Scotia

Association of Professional Engineers of Nova Scotia (APENS)
1355 Barrington Street, P.O. Box 129
Halifax NS B3J 2M4
Canada

Tel.: (902) 429-2250 or 1-888-802-7367

Fax: (902) 423-9769
http://www.apens.ns.ca/

Ontario

Professional Engineers of Ontario (PEO)
25 Sheppard Avenue West, Suite 1000
Toronto ON M2N 6S9
Canada

Tel.: (416) 224-1100 or 1-800-339-3716
Fax: (416) 224-8168 or 1-800-268-0496
http://www.peo.on.ca/

Prince Edward Island

Association of Professional Engineers of Prince Edward Island (APEPEI)
549 North River Road
Charlottetown PE C1E 1J6
Canada

Tel.: (902) 566-1268
Fax: (902) 566-5551
http://www.apepei.com/

Québec

Ordre des ingénieurs du Québec (OIQ)
2020, rue University, 18e étage
Montréal QC H3A 2A5
Canada

Tel.: (514) 845-6141 or 1-800-461-6141
Fax: (514) 845-1833
http://www.oiq.qc.ca/

Saskatchewan

Association of Professional Engineers and Geoscientists of Saskatchewan (APEGS)
2255-13th Avenue, Suite 104

Regina SK S4P 0V6
Canada

Tel.: (306) 525-9547 or 1-800-500-9547
Fax: (306) 525-0851
http://www.apegs.sk.ca/

Yukon

Association of Professional Engineers of Yukon (APEY)
3106 Third Avenue, Suite 404, P.O. Box 4125
Whitehorse YT Y1A 5G1
Canada

Tel.: (867) 667-6727
Fax: (867) 668-2142
http://www.apey.yk.ca/

NOTE: Not all engineering graduates in Ontario are professional engineers
A professional engineer must have satisfied the requirements set by PEO to
earn a licence. However, you can work in engineering without a licence, if a
professional engineer supervises and takes responsibility for your work. You
cannot use the title "professional engineer", the abbreviation "P.Eng.", o
any similar title that may lead to the belief that you are qualified to practise
professional engineering unless you are a licensed professional engineer.

Information on assessment of qualifications

For immigration purposes only, to any province or territory except
Quebec, you can obtain an assessment of your engineering
qualifications prior to your arrival from the Canadian Council of
Professional Engineers (CCPE). You may consult online the information
prepared by the Canadian Council of Professional Engineers in this
regard.

Canadian Council of Professional Engineers (CCPE)
180 Elgin Street, Suite 1100
Ottawa, Ontario K2P 2K3
Canada

Tel.: (613) 232-2474
Fax: (613) 236-5759

Email: ia@ccpe.ca
http://www.ccpe.ca/

Rev. Date: 2/19/2002 11:52:27 AM

For immigration to Quebec, you should contact the Ordre des ingénieurs du Québec (OIQ):

Ordre des ingénieurs du Québec (OIQ)
2020, rue University, 18e étage
Montréal, Québec H3A 2A5
Canada

Tel.: (514) 845-6141 or 1-800-461-6141
Fax: (514) 845-1833

Email: admission@oiq.qc.ca
http://www.oiq.qc.ca/
Rev. Date: 2/19/2002 12:12:39 PM

Please note that both OIQ and CCPE charge a fee for their services, and that their assessments **do NOT guarantee** recognition of your credentials for purposes of employment or licensure/certification in Canada.

You may also consult Fact Sheet No. 2, which has been compiled to help individuals learn more about how to obtain an assessment of their qualifications for employment purposes in Canada.

FACT SHEET No. 2

Assessment and recognition of credentials for the purpose of employment in Canada

Most individuals who plan to come to Canada to settle permanently and who wish to enter the labour force will need to know the value of the education, training, and experience they have acquired outside Canada. This fact sheet answers the most frequently asked questions about the process so that it may help individuals learn more about how to obtain assessment and recognition of their qualifications. Individuals intending to continue their education in Canada can learn more about the process by consulting **CICIC's Fact Sheet No. 1**, *Information for students educated abroad applying for admission to Canadian universities and colleges.* Both fact sheets are available in French and may be obtained by contacting CICIC directly or through its Web site (addresses listed under question 13).

1. *How can I get my qualifications obtained abroad recognized in Canada?*

The procedures for evaluating and recognizing qualifications earned outside Canada **will depend on** whether you wish to **enter an occupation** or **pursue further studies**, whether your chosen occupation is **regulated or non-regulated**, and the **province/territory** in which you intend to settle. For the purpose of this document, occupations will refer to both professions and trades. As a general rule, if your chosen occupation is regulated, the recognition of qualifications will be determined by the appropriate provincial or territorial regulatory body, while for a non-regulated occupation, recognition is normally at the discretion of the employer.

2. *What is the difference between a regulated and a non-regulated occupation?*

A **"regulated"** occupation is one that is controlled by provincial and territorial (and sometimes federal) law and governed by a professional organization or regulatory body. The **regulatory body** governing the profession/trade has the **authority** to set entry requirements and standards of practice, to assess applicants' qualifications and credentials, to certify, register, or license qualified applicants, and to discipline members of the profession/trade. Requirements for entry, which may **vary from one province to another**, usually consist of such components as examinations, a specified period of supervised work experience, language competency, etc. If you want to work in a regulated occupation and use a regulated title, **you MUST have a licence or certificate or be registered** with the regulatory body for your occupation. Some occupations are regulated in certain provinces and territories and are not regulated in others.

About 20 per cent of Canadians work in regulated occupations such as veterinarian, electrician, plumber, physiotherapist, medical doctor, engineer, etc. The system of regulation is intended to protect the health and safety of Canadians by ensuring that professionals meet the required standards of practice and competence.

A **"non-regulated"** occupation is a profession/trade for which there is **no legal requirement or restriction** on practice with regard to licences, certificates, or registration. **The vast majority of occupations** in Canada fall into this category. For some non-

186

regulated occupations, certification/registration with a professional body is available to applicants on a voluntary basis, whereas for other non-regulated occupations there is no certification/registration available at all.

In general, applicants for non-regulated occupations will have to demonstrate to their potential employers that they possess the experience and training required for the job. Even when an occupation is not regulated, employers can still require that an applicant for a job be registered, licensed, or certified with the relevant professional association.

3. *If I want to work in a regulated occupation, what can I do to get my qualifications assessed and recognized?*

Each regulated occupation sets its own requirements for assessment and recognition, usually through the **provincial or territorial professional association or regulatory body.** (In some cases, there are federal requirements for recognition.) In order to qualify for practice in Canada, you may be required to undergo professional and language examinations, submit to a review of your qualifications, and undertake a period of supervised work experience. You can find out more about the specific requirements for recognition of your qualifications in your profession/trade by doing the following:

1. Contact the professional association governing your occupation in **your own country** to find out if there are any links with similar associations in Canada. Consult the publication entitled National Occupational Classification at the closest Canadian diplomatic mission to find out more about employment requirements for your occupation.

2. Find out the name and address of the professional regulatory body governing your profession/trade in the province or territory where you intend to settle by enquiring with CICIC.

3. Write to the regulatory body and ask about the specific requirements and costs for licensing, certification, or registration, as well as the recommended procedure for an assessment. The regulatory body will advise you concerning the required documentation and the fees for assessment.

You should be aware that the recognition process is different in each province and territory and for each profession/trade. It can be a costly and time-consuming process; so it is important that you obtain all the information you need to know about the process and specific requirements before undertaking an assessment.

4. *If I want to work in a non-regulated occupation, what can I do to get my qualifications assessed and recognized?*

For a **non-regulated occupation**, requirements for employment can vary from very specific to very general. You may be expected to demonstrate a certain level of skill and competence, to have completed a certain number of years of education, and even to have personal characteristics suitable for the job. Since these requirements are **not regulated by provincial or territorial law**, it is up to the **employer to decide** whether your qualifications earned outside Canada are equivalent to Canadian credentials required for the occupation. Because registration and certification may be available for certain non-regulated occupations, some employers will require, as a condition for employment, that applicants be registered or certified by the relevant professional association.

There is no single process in place for the assessment of qualifications for purposes of entry into non-regulated occupations. However, there are several ways an applicant can try to facilitate the process for a potential employer.

o Get in touch with the association or organization relevant to your occupation in your home country and in Canada. Find out about the procedures recommended for an assessment of your qualifications. CICIC can direct you to the relevant organization in Canada, if one exists.

o Contact employers in your area of work experience to find out what the general expectations are for employment in Canada. Consult the publication entitled <u>National Occupational Classification</u>. A copy is available at the nearest <u>Canadian diplomatic mission</u>. Verify if there is voluntary certification or registration available and what the requirements are for the province or territory where you intend to work. To determine if there is a provincial agency providing certification in your particular occupation, visit the relevant page listed on <u>http://www.cicic.ca/professions/indexe.stm</u>

o If there are no provincial agencies, then contact one of the evaluation services listed below for an assessment of your credentials. Although these services offer **expert advice** on how qualifications obtained abroad compare with credentials obtained in a Canadian province or territory, the evaluation is advisory only and **does not guarantee** recognition of your qualifications for employment or certification purposes in Canada. However, it will assist employers, post-secondary institutions, and professional bodies in understanding your academic background. Please note that these agencies charge a fee for their services.

Provincially-mandated Evaluation Services

Alberta

International Qualifications Assessment Service

Alberta Learning
4th Floor, Sterling Place
9940 - 106 Street
Edmonton, Alberta   T5K 2V1   Canada

Tel: (780) 427-2655; Fax: (780) 422-9734
E-mail: iqas@gov.ab.ca
http://www.learning.gov.ab.ca/iqas/iqas.asp

British Columbia

International Credential Evaluation Service

4355 Mathissi Place
Burnaby, British Columbia   V5G 4S8   Canada

Tel: (604) 431-3402; Fax: (604) 431-3382
E-mail: ICES@ola.bc.ca
http://www.ola.bc.ca/ices/

Manitoba

Academic Credentials Assessment Service - Manitoba (ACAS)

Manitoba Labour and Immigration
Settlement & Labour Market Services Branch
5th Floor, 213 Notre Dame Avenue
Winnipeg, Manitoba, Canada R3B 1N3

Tel: (204) 945 - 6300 or (204) 945 - 5432
Fax: (204) 948 - 2148

E-mail: glloyd@gov.mb.ca
http://www.immigratemanitoba.com

Ontario

World Education Services-Canada

45 Charles Street East, Suite 700
Toronto, Ontario M4Y 1S2   Canada

Tel.: (416) 972-0070
Fax : (416) 972-9004
Toll-free: (866) 343-0070 (from outside the 416 area code)

Email: ontario@wes.org
http://www.wes.org/ca/

Quebec

Service des équivalences (SDE)

Ministère des Relations avec les citoyens et de l'Immigration
800, boulevard de Maisonneuve Est, 2e étage
Montréal (Québec) H2L 4L8   Canada

Tél : (514) 864-9191 ou (877) 264-6164; Fax : (514) 873-8701
Email: equivalences@mrci.gouv.qc.ca
http://www.immq.gouv.qc.ca/equivalences

Other Evaluation Services

Academic Credentials Evaluation Service

Office of Admissions, Room 150, Atkinson College

York University
4700 Keele Street
Toronto, Ontario M3J 1P3 Canada

Tel.: (416) 736-5787; Fax: (416) 736-5536
E-mail: dstadnic@yorku.ca
http://www.yorku.ca/admissio/aces.asp

Comparative Education Service

University of Toronto
315 Bloor Street West,
Toronto, Ontario M5S 1A3 Canada
Tel: (416) 978-2185; Fax: (416) 978-7022
http://www.adm.utoronto.ca/ces/

International Credential Assessment Service of Canada

147 Wyndham Street North, Suite 409
Guelph, ON
Canada   N1H 4E9

Tel: (519) 763-7282
Toll-free: (800) 321-6021
Fax : (519) 763-6964

Email: icas@sympatico.ca
http://www.icascanada.ca/

Evaluation services have an appeal process in place for individuals who wish to challenge the assessment of their credential.

1. *If I am applying for an immigration visa and need to know the value of my credentials, how can I get my credentials assessed prior to immigration?*

Although regulatory bodies will provide information on what is required to practise a profession or a trade, most regulatory bodies are not set up to assess foreign credentials prior to your arrival in Canada. Assessments are conducted by examinations and interviews, which means that you **MUST already be in Canada**. With very few exceptions, it is virtually impossible to obtain an assessment of credentials that would lead to eventual licensure, certification, or registration in the relevant occupation before you immigrate to Canada. Some regulated professions offer an initial assessment prior to immigration. Information can be obtained concerning this service by communicating directly with the regulatory body.

When a pre-immigration assessment is not available because the regulatory body does not offer it, or because your occupation is non-regulated, you can consult one of the credentials evaluation services listed under question 4. Although an assessment by one of these services does not guarantee recognition of your credentials for purposes of employment, licensure/certification, immigration, or further studies in Canada, it does provide an expert comparison of your qualifications with credentials obtained in a Canadian province or territory.

You should be aware that even if you meet the occupational requirements for immigration and are admitted to Canada, this, in itself, does not constitute a guarantee of employment. Acceptance for employment is a decision that rests solely with the employer.

2. *Where can I obtain a translation of my qualifications into English or French?*

If documents need to be translated, the evaluation service or regulatory body will advise you as to the requirements for translation and authentification of official documents.

3. *Is the university where I studied in my country recognized in Canada?*

Recognition of universities is the responsibility of the educational authorities of the country in which such institutions are located. Canadian evaluation services consult specialized tools such as the World Higher Education Database and the World Directory of National Information Centre for Academic Recognition and Mobility to determine if an institution is recognized. Recognition does not automatically mean that a given credential is automatically recognized in Canada. Other factors, such as national or provincial/territorial legislation and other specific requirements are considered in the evaluation of credentials and the licensing of professionals.

4. *What is a trade, and what is a* <u>*Red Seal*</u> *Trade?*

A trade is an occupation generally regarded as requiring one to three years of post-secondary education at a community college or university, two to four years of apprenticeship training, two to three years of on-the-job training, or a combination of these requirements. Some trades are regulated which means that a licence/certificate is required to practise in such cases.

Some trades are referred to as **Red Seal Trades.** A <u>Red Seal</u> Trade is a trade for which all the provinces and territories have agreed on standards for entry into the occupation allowing for the portability of qualifications across Canada. <u>Red Seal</u> Trades are designated by the Interprovincial Standards Program under the authority of the Canadian Council of Directors of Apprenticeship, the body that is also responsible for setting standards in the designated trades. The <u>Red Seal</u> is a passport that allows the holder to work anywhere in Canada without having to write further examinations.

In some provinces, certification is voluntary, meaning that neither a formal certificate nor a formal apprenticeship is required to practise the trade. However, the Red Seal Certificate would indicate that the holder has reached a certain level of expertise, and it may be required by some employers as a condition of employment. For a <u>list of designated Red Seal Trades</u> and the addresses of the <u>Provincial Apprenticeship Directors</u>, please contact <u>CICIC</u>.

5. *If I want an assessment of my credentials for my own information, how can I proceed?*

The best way to get an assessment of your credentials for information purposes is to consult one of the credentials evaluation services listed under <u>question 4</u> or, for licensing purposes, to contact the <u>appropriate professional regulatory body</u>.

Credential evaluation services offer expert advice about how your qualifications compare with credentials obtained in a Canadian province or territory; their evaluations are advisory only and **do not guarantee** recognition of your qualifications for immigration, further studies, employment, or licensure/certification purposes. However, this advice will assist employers, post-secondary institutions, and professional bodies in understanding your academic background. Please note that these agencies charge a fee for their services.

6. *Where can I learn more about employment opportunities in Canada?*

There is no central source of information about employment opportunities. **Please note that CICIC does not have information about employment opportunities.** **Once in Canada**, you can learn more about opportunities by contacting the **relevant professional associations**, reading the professional newsletters and bulletins, if available, and consulting the classified advertising section of the **local newspapers**. A number of **community and settlement organizations** also provide employment advice to newly arrived immigrants. In addition, many private employment agencies will help to place individuals. Some may charge a fee for this service.

Visit the various websites for job search like www.workopolis.ca

Labour market information

Job Futures:	http://www.jobfutures.ca/
Work Destinations:	http://www.workdestinations.ca/
Work*info*NET:	http://www.workinfonet.ca/
WorkSearch:	http://www.worksearch.gc.ca/

National Occupational Classification
http://cnp2001noc.worklogic.com/

7. *If I want to pursue further education in Canada, how do I get an assessment of my credentials?*

If you are thinking of studying in a Canadian college or university, contact the **office of admissions** of the institution in which you are interested and ask about the procedure required for an assessment of your credentials. The university or college has the sole authority to make decisions about recognition of credentials for purposes of admission. Individuals intending to continue their education in Canada can learn more about the process by consulting CICIC's Fact Sheet No. 1, *Information for students educated abroad applying for admission to Canadian universities and colleges.*

8. *What other sources of information are available?*

Immigration: general information and advice
to Canada : http://www.cic.gc.ca/

to Québec: http://www.immq.gouv.qc.ca/anglais/index.html

Post-secondary education in Canada
List of recognized institutions:
http://www.cicic.ca/postsec/indexe.stm

Company, business, and industry information
http://strategis.ic.gc.ca/

Reference Publications
Guide to Canadian terminology usage in the field of credential assessment and recognition
http://www.cicic.ca/pubs/guidtofb_en.stm

9. *What can CICIC do for me?*

The Canadian Information Centre for International Credentials (CICIC) assists persons who want to know how to obtain an assessment of their educational, professional, and occupational credentials by referring them to the appropriate bodies. **CICIC does not itself grant equivalencies or assess credentials, nor does it intervene on behalf of individuals or in appeals.** While colleges, universities, and licensing bodies have the sole authority to recognize foreign programs and degrees, CICIC fosters the dissemination of information about recognition procedures, promotes good and consistent practice in credentials assessment, and serves as a link for Canadian academic and professional bodies to international organizations and to similar institutions around the world.

CICIC collects data about procedures for recognizing academic and occupational credentials in different Canadian jurisdictions. This information is stored in a regularly updated database covering more than 800 professional, educational, and community agencies.

You are welcome to contact CICIC regarding qualifications assessment and recognition procedures by e-mail, telephone, fax, or post. Be sure to state in your enquiry the purpose for which you are seeking information on assessment, your intended occupation, and the province or territory where you plan to work.

Further information about post-secondary education and about other relevant organizations in Canada can be obtained by visiting the CICIC Web site: http://www.cicic.ca/

If you need further details, please do not hesitate to contact us again at the following address:

Canadian Information Centre for International Credentials

95 St. Clair Avenue West, Suite 1106
Toronto, Ontario M4V 1N6   Canada

Phone: (416) 962-9725
Fax: (416) 962-2800
Email: info@cicic.ca

Labour Market Information By Province And Territory

Canada is a large and diverse country. Job opportunities and labour market conditions are different in each region. It is important to obtain labour market information about the area where you want to live. Most provinces and territories provide information on their labour markets.

Alberta

Alberta Learning
7th Floor, Commerce Place
10155 102 Street
Edmonton, Alberta T5J 4L5

Telephone: 780-427-7219
Toll-free access, first dial 310-0000.
Fax: 780-422-1263

E-mail: comm.contact@learning.gov.ab.ca
URL: www.learning.gov.ab.ca/welcome/English/pdf/Employment.pdf

British Columbia

Aboriginal, Multiculturalism and Immigration Programs
PO Box 9214
Stn Prov Govt
Victoria, British Columbia V8W 9J1

Telephone: 250 952-6434
Fax: 250 356-5316
URL: www.gov.bc.ca/mi/popt/movingtobc.htm

Manitoba

Immigration and Multiculturalism Division
5th floor - 213 Notre Dame Avenue
Winnipeg, Manitoba R3B 1N3

Telephone: (204) 945-3162
Facsimile: (204) 948-2256

Email: immigratemanitoba@gov.mb.ca
URL: www.gov.mb.ca/labour/immigrate/newcomerservices/8.html

New Brunswick

Investment and Immigration,
Department of Business New Brunswick
P O Box 6000
Fredericton, New Brunswick E3B 5H1

Telephone: (506) 444-4640
Facsimile: (506) 444-4277

E-mail:immigration@gnb.ca
URL: www.gnb.ca/immigration/english/work/work.htm

Ontario

Access to Professions and Trades Unit
Ministry of Training, Colleges and Universities
12th Floor, 900 Bay Street, Mowat Block
Toronto, Ontario M7A 1L2

Telephone: (416) 326-9714
Facsimile: (416) 326-6265

E-mail: aptinfo@edu.gov.on.ca
URL: www.equalopportunity.on.ca/eng_g/apt/index.asp

Prince Edward Island

Immigration and Investment,
Development and Technology
94 Euston Street 2nd Floor
Charlottetown, PEI C1A 1W4

Telephone: (902) 894-0351
Facsimile: (902) 368-5886
URL: www.gov.pe.ca/infopei/Employment/index.php3

Quebec

Ministère des Relations avec les citoyens
et de l'Immigration (MRCI)

How to reach :

www.immigration-quebec.gouv.qc.ca/anglais/ reach.html

Email: Renseignements.DRM@mrci.gouv.qc.ca

URL: www.immigration-quebec.gouv.qc.ca/anglais/services/insertion_en.html

Saskatchewan

Saskatchewan Government Relations and Aboriginal Affairs
8th Floor, 1919 Saskatchewan Drive
Regina, Saskatchewan S4P 3V7

Email: immigration@iaa.gov.sk.ca

URL: www.iaa.gov.sk.ca/iga/immigration/Immigration.htm

(Accreditation and Services sites under development)

Yukon

Labour Market Program and Services -
Department of Education
Advanced Education Branch
Box 2703Whitehorse, Yukon Y1A 2C6

Telephone: (867) 667-5141 or
Toll Free: 800-661-0408
Facsimile: (867) 667-8555

LETS FIND A JOB

The first item on your line of action towards finding a job in Canada is to create a North American style resume (C.V). Visit various recruiters or job search websites listed in next section where you will find help to create your resume. Tailor your resume according to each job title and description you intend to apply for. Its worthwhile to spend few minutes every time you apply for a job. If the employer wants apples and oranges in the job description or experience of the candidate then you should incorporate both in your resume otherwise you may not get an interview call. So avoid mailing generic resume that may lead you to frustration. Following is an example of a North American style resume.

North American Style Resume

James Backer
101-1465 Lawrence Avenue E., Toronto, ON Z1R 2P8 ☎ (416) 798-1543 ✍
James_backer@hotmail.com

OBJECTIVE: Mechanical Project Engineer / Project Supervisor

SUMMARY OF QUALIFICATIONS

10+ years of international experience in the Electro-Mechanical Construction and Engineering industry especially in Oil/Gas sector. Broad knowledge base in engineering and project management. Competent in office management and accounting. **Well-groomed in EPCM environment** with problem solving abilities.

RELEVANT SKILLS AND EXPERIENCE

- Extensive experience and knowledge of ASME Codes.
- Proven management skills and record of accomplishment as per schedules.
- Management talent for "seeing the whole picture"
- Confident and decisive under stressful conditions,
- Effective in budgeting (managed up to $ 200,000) and cost control.
- Extensive experience in report writing and proposals
- Enthusiastic, committed, resourceful team player with exceptional communication & interpersonal skills.
- Self-motivated, Adaptable, Quick Learner.

SUMMARY OF COMPETENCIES

- Project Design & Management
- Engineering Management
- Estimating, Budgeting and P&L
- Resource Planning & Management
- Field Installation Management

- Client Presentations & Negotiation
- Cross-Functional Team Leadership
- Vendor Selection & Negotiation
- Material Selection & Management
- Product and Technology R&D

Excellent in client relationship management and cross-cultural communications. PC proficient with Microsoft Office Suit, MS Project Autocad Rel. 14/2000 and familiar with Primavera P3.

200

EDUCATION & PROFESSIONAL LISCENSE

- B.Sc Mechanical Engineering - 1991
- Professional Engineer **(P.Eng) - Ontario**

EMPLOYMENT HISTORY

Project Engineer - Alfa Constructions Inc. Toronto - 1995 to the present

Supervised a staff of 25+ professional and support personnel and completed various multi-billion $ projects in oil/gas and power sector

Supervisor – Sonic Engineering - Alberta 1992 to 1994

Supervised a staff of 30+ professional and support personnel and participated in a $4Billion underground fuel oil storage project. Completed 20-25 Kilometer of ½"-20" various services pressure piping installation and testing as per ASME Codes

TOP INTERVIEW QUESTIONS ASKED BY CANADIAN EMPLOYERS

1. Tell me about yourself?
2. Tell me about any of your weakness?
3. What are some of your strengths?
4. Where do you see yourself in 5 years?
5. What work experience have you had that prepares you for this position?
6. Why should we hire you?
7. Do you consider yourself a creative problem solver? Give me an example.
8. Why did you leave your last position?
9. Your resume shows you have moved around a lot. How can I be sure you will stay at this company?
10. What did you think of your last supervisor/manager?
11. Describe your ideal position.
12. What did you like about your last job?
13. What did you dislike about your last job?
14. Describe how you work under pressure.
15. Describe your ideal boss.
16. What do you have to offer this company that others may not?
17. What kind of salary are you looking for?
18. What was your annual salary at your last position?
19. What have you gained from working at your last job?
20. What were your responsibilities and duties?
21. What motivates you?
22. Do you consider yourself successful?
23. What traits or qualities do you most admire in someone?
24. What are your hobbies?
25. Are you willing to relocate?
26. Tell me about your proudest accomplishment?
27. What has been your most meaningful educational experience?
28. Can you tell me something about our company.
29. Describe how you perform in a high stress position?
30. How do you feel about routine work?
31. What steps are you taking to improve yourself?
32. Do you have a personal goal that you still want to achieve?
33. Tell me about what you would do to get organized for a project.
34. Have you ever been responsible for financial management?
35. There is a period of time on your resume when you were not employed. Can you tell me what you did in that time period?
36. Would it be appropriate to contact your most recent employer?
37. What do you think will be the most difficult aspect of this job?
38. What special skills / talents do you have?

39.   Do you have any questions for me? (usually at the end of interview)

Note: When you will visit your nearest Human Resource Centre in Canada, you will find many books on interview questions with their answers and some with specific professions. You will also find many books on resume writing.

INTERVIEW QUESTIONS BY DIFFERENT GROUPS

Your Past

1.   Why did you leave your last job?
2.   What aspects of your responsibilities did you consider most critical?
3.   What type of management did you have in your last job?
4.   Which job, of all the ones you have had, did you like the best? Why?
5.   Which job did you like the least? Why?
6.   What did you accomplish which benefited the company? The job?
7.   Where does this job fit in to your overall career plan?
8.   How do you organize for major projects?

What You Learned

1.   What special aspects of your education/training have prepared you for this job?
2.   In what area would you most like additional training if you do get this job?

Why you Learned

1.   What are your career goals?
2.   What kid of job do you see yourself holding in five years time? Why
3.   What would you most like to accomplish if you get this job?
4.   What do you consider your biggest career success to date?

Type of Jobs & Your Style

1.   Tell me about one of your favourite work experiences. What did you like best about it.
2.   How do you know when you have done a good job.
3.   How did your past supervisor evaluate your performance? What areas of improvement were suggested?
4.   Why do you feel that you are qualified for this position?

Stress Management

1.   Tell me about a work situation that gave you difficulty?
2.   Define co-operation.

Strengths

1.   What key factors have accounted for your career success to date?
2.   In what areas have others been particularly complimentary about your abilities?

Weakness

1.   What do you think your co-workers would view as your greatest weakness?

Interpersonal Skills.

1.   What sorts of people do you have difficulty working with?
2.   With which of your past work groups did you most enjoy working?
3.   What factors most influenced your positive feelings.
4.   With which of your past work groups did you least enjoy working? What accounted for that, what did you do about it and what was the outcome?
5.   What aspects of your interpersonal skills would you like most to improve?
6.   Tell me about a confrontational situation at work. How did you handle it?

Type of Work you Like

1.   What type of work do you find most stimulating and rewarding? Why? Least stimulating? Why?
2.   In which of your last positions were you most motivated and productive?
3.   What has your experience taught you about the type of work you least enjoy?
4.   What factors contributed the most to your job dissatisfaction?

Your Preferred work Environment

1.   In which of your past work environments (team, independent) were you the happiest? Why?
2.   In which of your past work environments did you feel you had the greatest amount of influence and impact?
3.   How would you describe the ideal work environment? Which things would be present? Which things would be absent?

Traits and Characteristics

1. What word best describes your personal style?
2. Which of your personal traits has been most helpful in your career?
3. If 3 of your close associates were here, what would they say about you?

Business Philosophy

1. How do you think successful businesses manage their employees.

Your Operating Style

1. How would you categorize your operating style (the way you go about your business/work?)
2. What are the basic work principles by which you operate?

Overcoming Rejections & Objections

1. You're overqualified!
2. We're looking for someone a little younger/older!
3. All hiring is done by personnel/we're supposed to go through personnel with these things!
4. We're cutting back right now. Why don't you call in three months/we're actually laying people off right now!
5. I'd love to see you, but I'm tied up in a meeting!

INTERVIEW PRACTICE – AN EXAMPLE

Practicing for the interview means practicing several behaviours – not just answering questions. You must dress well, watch your body language and posture, practice your manners and eye contact, as well as practice answering questions correctly, smoothly and with confidence.

The practice questions below, in one form or another, account for a large percentage of interview questions. With each question, you are given a series of choices as to how you might answer the question. When you select an answer, you will learn to whether your answer is correct or not - and why. Answering these questions will help you polish your interviewing techniques. The questions and answers in this exercise are generic and in many cases, must be tailored to your individual situation. Still, the logic behind the answer remains essentially the same.

1.   Why are you the best person for the job?

(a)   "I've held a lot of positions like this one and that experience will help me here."

(b)   "Because I am good at what I do."

(c)   "Our discussion here leads me to believe this is a good place to work."

(d)   "You need someone who can produce results and my background and experience are proof of my ability. For example..."

2.   If asked a point blank question such as : Are you creative? Are you analytical? Can you work under pressure? Etc. what is the best way to answer?

(a)   Answer yes or no.

(b)   Answer yes and give a specific example.

(c)   Answer yes and give an explanation.

3.   Describe yourself.

(a)   Outline personal data, hobbies and interests.

(b)   Give an overview of your personality and work habits.

(c)   Give three specific examples of your personality traits and accomplishments.

4.   Why are you in the job market?

(a)   "I have invested a great deal of time with my company and become disenchanted with the ways things are done".

(b)   "I have a solid plan for my career. Within that plan I am looking fo
additional responsibility and more room for growth."

(c)   "I have been passed over for promotions when I know I am capable
of doing
more. I want to move on to a company that will not stunt my growth.

LIST OF SUGGESTED JOB SEARCH WEB SITES

Canada Job search	www.canadajobsearch.com
Canada Wide	www.canada.com
Canada Work Info Net (B)	http://workinfonet.ca
Canada Work Infonet	www.workinfonet.com
Canadian Career Page	www.canadiancareers.com
Career Bookmarks	www.careerbookmarks.tpl.toronto.on.ca
Career Exchange	www.creerexchange.com
Career Mosaic	www.careermosaic.com
Career Networking	www.careerkey.com
Contractors Network Corporation	www.cnc.ca
Culture Net Announcement Board	www.culturenet.ca
Electronic Labour Exchange	www.ele-spe.org
E-Span	www.espan.com
Head Hunter	www.HeadHunter.net
HEART/Career Connections	www.career.com
Hot Jobs	www.hotjobs.com
HRDC Canada(B)	www.hrdc-drhc.gc.ca
Job Bus Canada	www.jobbus.com
Job Find	www.jobfind2000.com
Job Hunters Bible	www.jobhuntersbible.com
Job Search Canada	www.jobsearchcanada.about.com
Job Search Engine	www.job-search-engine.com
Job Shark	www.jobshark.com
Monster Board	www.monster.ca
Net Jobs	www.netjobs.com
Ontario Government (B)	www.gojobs.gov.on.ca
Public Service Commission of Canada(B)	http://jobs.gc.ca
SERN	www.sern.net
Toronto HRDC Jobs and Links	www.toronto-hrdc.sto.org
Toronto Job Ads	www.workwaves.com
University of Toronto Job Board	www.utoronto.ca/jobopps
Work Search (B)	www.worksearch.gc.ca
Workink(B)	www.workink.com
Work Insight	www.workinsight.com
Workopolis	www.workopolis.com

HI TECH

Hi Tech Career Exchanges	www.hitechcareer.com

IT Career Solutions	www.vectortech.com
Position Watch	www.positionwatch.com
Ward Associates	www.ward-associates.com

ENGINEERING

Canadian Society for Mechanical Engineers	www.csme.ca
Engineering Institute of Canada	www.eic.ici.ca

NON PROFIT ORGANIZATION

Canadian International Development Agency	www.acdi-cida.gc.ca
Charity Village	www.charityvillage.com
Human Rights-Job Bank	www.Hri.ca/jobboard/joblinks.shtml
Law Now's Resource for Charity/Non Profit	www.extension.ualberta.ca/lawnow/nfp
Online Resource for Non Profit	www.onestep.on.ca

HEALTH

Canadian Medical Placement Service	www.cmps.ca
Hospital News	www.hospitalnews.com
Med Hunters	www.medhunters.com

EDUCATION

Jobs in the Educational Field	www.oise.utoronto.ca/~mpress/jobs.html

WOMEN

Wired Women	www.wiredwoman.com

MULTI MEDIA

MultiMediator	www.multimediator.com

TOURISM AND HOSPITALITY

Cool Jobs Canada	www.cooljobscanada.com
Hospitality Careers	www.hcareers.com

AGRICULTURE

Caffeine	www.caffeine.ca
The Farm Directory	www.farmdirectory.com/employment.asp

ARTS AND ENTERTAINMENT

Acting	www.madscreenwriter.com
ACTRA (film)	www.actra.com

Canadian Actor Online	www.canadianactor.com
Canadian Actors Equity Association	www.caea.com
Canadian film @ TV Production Association	www.cftpa.ca
Canadian Film Centre	www.cdnfilmcentre.com
Mandy	www.mandy.com
National Film Board	www.nfb.ca
Ontario Theatre	www.theatreontario.org
Playback Magazine	www.playbackmag.com

SPECIALIZED

Canadian Federation of Chefs & Cooks	www.cfcc.ca
Canadian Human Resource Counsellors	www.chrp.ca
Contact Point – Counsellors	www.contactpoint.ca
Oil and Gas Industry	www.pcf.ab.ca
Social Workers of Toronto	www.swatjobs.com

PEOPLE WITH DISABILITIES

Canadian Council for Rehabilitation & Work	www.ccrw.org
Canadian Hearing Society	www.chs.ca
Canadian Mental health Association	www.cmha.ca
Canadian Paraplegic Association	www.canparaplegic.org
Job Accommodation Network	http://janweb.icdi.wvu.edu
TCG for People with Disabilities	www.tcg.on.ca
U of T Adaptive Tech ERC	www.utoronto.ca/atrc

WEB SITES FOR YOUTH AND RECENT GRADUATES

Bridges	www.bridges.com
Canadian Youth Business Foundation	www.cybf.ca
Canadian Youth Business Foundation (B)	www.cybf.ca
Career Owl	www.careerowl.ca
Career Planning	www.alis.gov.ab.ca
Cdn.International Development Agency(B)	www.acdi-cida.gc.ca
Fedeal Student Work Experience Program (B)	www.jobs.gc.ca
MazeMaster	www.mazemaster.on.ca
National Graduate Register	http://ngr.schoolnet.ca
Strategies Business Info – By Sector (B)	Strategis.ic.gc.ca/sc_indps/en gdoc/homepage.html
Summer Jobs	www.summerjobs.com
Work Web (B)	www.cacee.com
Youth Canada (B)	www.youth.gc.ca
Youth Info-Job (B)	www.infojob.net
Youth Opportunities Ontario (B)	Youthjobs.gov.on.ca
Youth Opportunities Ontario (B)	www.edu.gov.on.ca

NEW COMERS

Citizenship and Immigration Canada	www.cic.gc.ca
Settlement.org	www.sttlement.org
Skills for change	www.skillsforchange.org
World Educational Services/Foreign Credentials Assessment	www.wes.org/ca

CAREER PLANNING AND JOB SEARCH STRATEGIES

Bridges	www.cxbridges.com
Career Cruising	www.careercruising.com
Counsellor Resource Centre (B)	http://crccanada.org
Essential Skills	www.essestialskills.gc.ca
Job Futures	http://jobfutures.ca
National Occupational Classification (NOC)(B)	www.hrdc.gc.ca/noc
Toronto Public Library	http://careerbookmarks.tpl.vrl.toronto.on.ca
What Colour is your parachute:	www.jobhuntersbible.com

LABOUR MARKET / INDUSTRY INFORMATION

Canada News Wire	www.newswire.ca
Canada Work InfoNet (B)	www.workinfonet.ca
HRDC Metro Toronto(B)	www.toronto-hrdc.sto.org
HRDC Sector Studies (B)	www.on.hrdc-drhc.gc.ca/english/lmi
Industry Canada	http://strategis.ic.gc.ca
Labour Market Information: Salary Ranges	www.Canadavisa.com/documents/salary.htm
Ontario Wage Information	www.on.hrdc-drhc.gc.ca
Workwaves Toronto	www.workwaves.com

NEWSPAPERS/MAGAZINE

Eye Magazine	www.eye.net/classifieds.
Globe and Mail	www.theglobeandmail.com
National Post	www.careerclick.com
Newswire	www.neweswire.ca
Toronto Star	www.thestar.com
Toronto Star / Globe and Mail	www.workpolis.com
Toronto Sun	www.canoe.ca

SMALL BUSINESS INFORMATION

Business Development Bank of Canada (B)	www.bdc.ca
Canada Business Service Centres	www.cbsc.org

(B)	
Canadian Company Capabilities (B)	Strategis.ic.gc.ca/engdoc/main.htm l
Canadian Women's business Network	www.cdnbizwomen.com
Educated Entrepreneur	www.educatedentrepreneur.com
Enterprise Toronto	www.enterprisetronto.com
Self Employment Assistance	http://www.sedi.org/html/prog/fs1_ prog.html
Toronto Business	www.city.toronto.on.ca/business/in dex.htm

WEB SITES WHERE YOU CAN POST YOUR RESUME

Electronic Labour Exchange	www.ele-spc.org
Job Canada	www.jobcanada.org
Job Shark (B)	www.jobshark.com
Monster Board (B)	www.monster.ca
National Graduate Register (B)	www.campusworklink.com
NetJobs	www.netjobs.com
Worklink	www.workink.com
Workopolis	www.workopolis.ca

TRAINING

Can Learn	www.canlearn.ca
Ellis Chart/Apprentice Training Programs	www.hrdc.gc.ca/hrib/hrpprh/redseal/ ndex.shtml
Interactive Training Inventory (B)	www.trainingiti.com
Ministry of Eduction & Training	www.edu.gov.on.ca/eng/welcome.ht ml
Onestep	www.onestep.on.ca
Ontario Universities' Application Centre	www.ouac.on.ca
Scholarships and Exchanges (B)	www.homer.aucc.ca
School finder(B)	www.schoolfinder.com

TUTORIAL SITES

Internet Stuff	www.webteacher.com
Learn the Net	www.learnthenet.com
Microsoft Office: word, excel, powerpoint	www.utexax.edu/cc/training/handouts
Mouse Tutorial	www.albright.org/Albright/computer-Lab/tutorials/mouse/

RELEVANT INFORMATION

City of Toronto	www.city.toronto.on.ca

213

Employment Resource Centres	www.tcet.com/ercs
Possibilities Project	www.possibilitiesproject.com

VOLUNTEER SITES

Charity Village	www.charityvillage.com
Rehabilitation	www.voc-reb.org
Volunteers	www.volunteer.ca

FREE EMAILS SITES

Excite	www.excite.com
Hotmail	www.hotmail.com
Mail City	www.mailcity.com
Yahoo	www.yahoo.com

SINGLE SEARCH ENGINES

www.google.com	www.altavista.com
www.excite.com	www.go.com
www.hotbot.com	www.yahoo.ca

META SEARCH ENGINES

www.search.com	www.profusion.com
www.megaweb.com	www.metacrawler.com
www.dogpile.com	

TIPS:

- Post your resume on-line where ever possible and register with as many recruiting agencies as you can. Services of these agencies are free for candidates because they are being paid by the employer if they find them an employee of their choice.

- Your resume should not be more then 2 pages of MS Word. The average time spent by an employer in Canada to shortlist resume is 10-15 seconds.

- Access your resume by response, If you apply against 100 jobs and you receive 3-5 interviews that mean your resume is fine and you are doing a good job.

- After arriving in Canada attend job search workshops and trainings organized by your nearest HRDC (Human Resource Development Canada) office free of charge. You will learn how job search techniques are different in Canada from rest of the world.

- When you are in Canada, do your networking, let as many people know as possible that you are looking for a job and learn making cold calls. These are the highly successful and result oriented methods of job search in Canada.

- Mail at least 5-10 resume and 5 cold calls everyday for quick results.

- www.workopolis.com, www.monster.ca & www.hotjobs.com are the most commonly used websites for job search.

Some Useful Toll-Free Numbers
Form USA and Canada only

Information on the Government of Canada	1 800 622-6232
Canada Business Service Centres	1 800 576-4444
Canada Child Tax Benefit	1800 387-1193
Canada Education Saving Grant	1 888 276-3624
Canada Saving Bonds	1 800 575-5151
Citizenship and Immigration Canada	
In Montreal (local call)	1 54 496-1010
In Toronto (local call)	1 416 973-4444
In Vancouver (local call)	1 604 666-2171
Elsewhere in Canada	1 888 242-2100
Customs Information Service	1 800 461-9999
Employment Insurance and Social Insurance Number	1 800 206-7218
Old Age Security and Canada Pension plan	1 800 277-9914
Passport Office	1 800567-6868
Tax Enquiries-personal	1 800 959-8281
Youth Info Line	1 800 935-5555

About the Author

The Author is a Mechanical Engineer and Cisco Certified Network and Design professional (CCNP, CCDP, A+) with more then 14 years of experience in his field of expertise with multi-national companies especially in Middle East. He arrived in Canada as an immigrant and faced numerous surprises and challenges as well as suffering a number of losses.

The Author has a flare to help and teach, he wishes to save new immigrants from potential losses and miseries by sharing the wealth of information that he has gathered while immigrating and settling in Canada. After interviewing hundreds of new immigrants from various countries, the author has come to the conclusion that the root cause of all the problems and loss of hard earned money is the lack of information before arriving in Canada.

So by compiling this publication he is giving everything to new or potential immigrants to not only prepare and submit their immigration application under skilled worker class in a professional manner but to start working towards their eligibility for employment in Canada and explore or secure a job offer while their cases are in process.

The Author can be reached at *tariq_nadeem@sympatico.ca* for advise or feedback upon his publication.

He has compiled this publication with the approval of Citizenship and Immigration Canada (CIC) and with the authorization of Communication Canada, Ottawa, Ontario K1A 1M4

Printed in the United Kingdom
by Lightning Source UK Ltd.
116936UKS00001B/309